naturally modern

naturally modern

CREATING INTERIORS WITH WOOD, STONE, LEATHER, AND NATURAL FABRICS

Ros Byam Shaw

photography by ANDREW WOOD

Harry N. Abrams, Inc., Publishers

Senior designer Paul Tilby
Senior editor Annabel Morgan
Location research manager Kate Brunt
Location researcher Sarah Hepworth
Production Patricia Harrington
Art director Gabriella Le Grazie
Publishing director Alison Starling

Library of Congress Cataloging-in-Publication
Data

Byam Shaw, Ros.
    Naturally modern : creating sophisticated
interiors with wood, stone, leather, and natural
fabrics / Ros Byam Shaw ; photography by
Andrew Wood.
            p. cm.
    Includes bibliographical references and index.
    ISBN 0-8109-3668-2
    1. Interior decoration-Themes, motives. I. Title
    NK2113 B93 2000
    747-dc21
                        00-029316

Harry N. Abrams, Inc.
100 Fifth Avenue
New York, N.Y. 10011
www.abramsbooks.com

contents

OPPOSITE PAGE: A chain-mail fire guard, a stone hearth, and a beautifully sculptural log make a focal point between living and dining rooms in a house in the Hollywood Hills. Forming a low window in the brick wall that divides them, the fireplace draws the two rooms together like the central hearth of a great Medieval hall.

LEFT AND FAR LEFT: Wood, linen, wool, and leather working together in Roger Oates' and Fay Morgan's Georgian country house. An antique linen sheet dresses the sofa for summer and a child's wooden high chair makes a perfect lamp stand.

BELOW: A detail of the monumental chimney breast and hefty mantel in a house in Idaho by architect Mark Pynn. Internal exposed stone walling in local "Trail Creek" stone and a lavish use of American hardwoods give the interior the rugged, sturdy feel of a craftsman-made vernacular building. The checkerboard trim reappears at the corners of window casings throughout the house.

introduction

Natural materials—wood, leather, stone, and natural fibers—occupy a special place in the human psyche. Like the threads of ritual and tradition that bind us to our past, the raw materials of our ancestors—the stone of caves and circles, the wood of huts and firelight, the skins of our first clothing—are things we find beautiful almost by instinct.

Over the centuries, man has worked on transforming these God-given staples to extraordinary effect—chiseling marble to the silk of human flesh, carving wood into lace, gilding and embossing leather until it resembles cast metal. In this last century we have gone farther, manipulating nature's very building blocks to make entirely new materials, so comprehensively processed it is almost impossible to guess their origins—animal, vegetable, or mineral.

In a world dominated by technology, raw nature has never seemed more alluring. Life is complicated, plastic, computerized. But, within the walls of our own homes, we can create a haven that brings us back in touch with fundamental pleasures—the comforting solidity of stone, the gentle grain of wood, the faint, clean animal scent of tanned leather, the tender brush of cashmere.

This powerful pull of the natural goes with a taste for interiors that minimize clutter and accentuate sensual appeal. "Honest" craftsmanship, with its distaste for the overwrought, is back in fashion, and the words of Victorian proponents of the Arts and Crafts movement, who were themselves in reaction against mass production and fussy ornament, again ring true. "Employ only those forms and materials which make for simplicity, individuality and dignity of effect," urged American furniture maker and theorist, Gustav Stickley. Architect and designer Charles Voysey spoke for them all when he opined "Carving richly veined marbles and finely figured wood is only the action of irreverence and conceit. We ought to respect nature's veining too much to allow of our chopping it up with man-made pattern."

After the chintzy excesses of the 1980s and the rigor of cutting-edge minimalism, we seem to be finding a middle ground much in the Arts and Crafts tradition where natural materials speak for themselves, and comfort and fashion co-exist. As the houses in this book illustrate, a modern interior need be neither cold nor sterile. "Nature's veining," nature's colors and textures, bring a warmth and intimacy to all rooms and a look that will wear, weather, and last beyond the vagaries of fashion.

> "In a world dominated by technology, nature has never seemed more alluring."

ABOVE LEFT AND OPPOSITE PAGE: Designer Aude Cardinale has transformed the concrete volumes of a saucepan factory in Paris into a house of sophisticated luxury. The double-height salon (opposite) is floored in mottled brown limestone and furnished with chairs and a sofa upholstered in velvety nubuck leather. Concrete beams (above left) have been painted to look like wood, and the generous folds of floor-to-ceiling curtains bring an atmosphere of warmth and softness to spaces that once rattled with heavy machinery. LEFT: Natural woods never clash: cedar Venetian blinds fall to a floor of bleached teak.

elements

Touching wood for luck is rarely difficult. Wood is so remarkably versatile that we are usually within touching distance of at least one of its products, whether matchstick or newspaper. Familiar, even mundane, the stuff of coffins and galleons, of bridges and baseball bats, of railroad ties and pencils, wood is also one of the most beautiful and practical materials available to the architect and interior designer, used structurally, decoratively, or, in the best Arts and Crafts tradition, as a combination of the two.

Like the water or earth from which it springs, the tree is crucial to our environment and our wellbeing. Trees anchor the soil, binding it together with their network of roots, preventing erosion. Trees provide shelter from the sun and a shield from the wind. Trees make homes for birds, insects, and fungi. Trees use carbon dioxide to photosynthesize, excreting oxygen as a waste product. Gathered in their hundreds of thousands, whether as tropical rainforest or temperate and broad-leaved forests, there is growing evidence that trees influence not only local climatic conditions, but the weather of the world.

As if in unconscious recognition of their benevolent role, trees have been revered, even worshipped, since ancient times. Trees and groves were sacred to the Greeks, who associated particular species with particular gods: the oak with Zeus, the olive with Athena, and the laurel with Apollo. The powerful symbolism of the tree, its roots pushing deep underground, its branches reaching toward the sky, its canopy a shelter, its trunk a pillar of strength, was represented in Norse legend by the Yggdrasil, a giant ash tree binding regions of heaven and hell, with the earth sandwiched between the two.

LEFT: Like the ripples in sand, the grain of wood has the suggestive power of an abstract painting. This burl oak veneer covers floor-to-ceiling kitchen cabinets in a London apartment.

wood

THIS PAGE: Wood in some of its many guises: supple and sophisticated for a contemporary chair (left and below), strong and handsome for an Arts and Crafts house (right), calm and collected in a modern interior (below left). Wood can also be carved and persuaded into all manner of shapes and forms. The gently curved back rails of the Arts and Crafts chairs (right) have been steam-bent, while the swooping arms and front leg of the Sawaya and Moroni chair (left) are thanks to the malleability of plywood.

Even without the gloss of any religious or spiritual associations, trees are awe-inspiring objects: towering above us, flexing in the wind, stoutly powerful where they meet the ground, tapering toward their extremities into twigs to create winter silhouettes that are as delicate as lace. From a distance their summer leaves present an infinite variety of downy green, an illusion of softness that resolves with proximity into an intricate and spiky tracery of twig and branch. Bare or clothed, palest emerald in spring, fiery red or orange in autumn, the deciduous tree is nature's visual clock. In terms of longevity, as well as size, man is a midget compared with a tree. To plant one is to leave a legacy that may be enjoyed by great-great-great-grandchildren. While generations are born and buried, trees look on, inching outward and upward, losing and gaining branches, living through hundreds, perhaps even thousands, of winters and summers, springs and falls.

As the legacy of these great living plants, wood carries with it many of the virtues and attributes of the tree from which it has been carved. Just as no two trees are identical, so every piece of wood has its own unique fingerprint, an infinite and fascinating lack of uniformity that gives each and every wooden floor, table, or piece of paneling its own particular character and identity. Wood has remarkable dual tendencies: it is strong, rigid with the effort of keeping the weight of leaves and branch erect, and yet also flexible and effective under both compression and tension.

OPPOSITE PAGE: Certain types of wood have quite distinct images—pine is kitchen tables and Swedish saunas, maple is butchers' blocks and expanses of pale flooring in chic modern apartments, mahogany is regency chests. Oak, with its reputation for strength and associations with an "honest" homespun style of vernacular architecture and furniture, was the chosen medium of the Arts and Crafts furniture makers, who used it to make simple, elegant pieces like this slat-back dining chair.

LEFT: Old wood and new, English and African, happily cohabit in the kitchen and living room of this nineteenth-century townhouse. The low bench is African and carved from dark wenge wood.
INSET LEFT: Sanded plywood makes attractive and inexpensive flooring in a converted warehouse.
OPPOSITE PAGE: A woody effect with little real wood in this Paris apartment. The furniture is cane and bamboo, while pillars and beams owe their appearance to paint effects.

Living trees must defend themselves against attack by rot and insect. Beneath the protective skin of bark, trees have numerous in-built defenses: resins that act as insecticides, fungicides, and waterproofing and which even continue to work after the tree has been felled. Some woods, such as teak, are particularly rich in these natural preservatives. Locust and iron wood are so impervious to damp and rot that their logs can be sunk straight into the earth and remain intact. In Malaysia, houses built on stilts of iron wood remain sturdy for generations – a feat of endurance that would test the most sophisticated of man-made construction materials.

There are tens of thousands of different species of tree, and new species are still being discovered. The range of uses man puts them to is commensurately vast. Aside from wood in all its forms, including pulp for paper and cardboard, charcoal, plywood, chipboard and MDF (medium-density fiberboard), trees provide food, medicines, cork, rubber, gum, syrup, glue, turpentine, and latex. Trees are victims of their extraordinary versatility as raw material.

Before man began his chopping and burning, a blanket of forest wrapped much of the world. Today, half of that original tropical rainforest and three-quarters of the ancient temperate forests have vanished, mostly up in smoke, either burned as they stand to make way for agriculture and grazing, or chopped into logs for heating and cooking. As creeping deforestation continues to eat into the wild woodlands and jungles of the world, we have come to see trees as more than a resource for our consumption, or a nuisance to be cleared, and to recognize their vital role in the delicate natural balance of our planet.

A knee-jerk reaction to fears about the long-term health of the environment might be to assume that we should use as little wood in our homes as possible, laying vinyl floors instead of boards, or choosing metal or plastic for our furnishings. Indeed, some valuable hardwoods, such as rosewood from the dalbergia tree, hugely fashionable for fine furniture throughout much of the nineteenth century and imported to Europe from South America and the West Indies, are unobtainable today, having been exhausted by ferocious demand. Perhaps a contemporary

" *A material used by man since ancient times, wood still looks modern and sassy.* "

THIS PAGE AND OPPOSITE
ABOVE: Wooden wall
paneling has been in use
since the Middle Ages,
popular for its insulating
properties as much as for
its decorative merits.
Contemporary versions of
paneling, like the iroko
planks lining the walls in
this London apartment
(left and above) and the
redwood that sweeps
around the rooms of a
house in the Hollywood
Hills (above right), place
their emphasis on the
aesthetics of wooden walls,
rejoicing in its color and
grain. Neither of these
modern homes needs
extra insulation, but the
psychological effect of the
paneling is as warming
and comforting as ever.

> **The dark good looks of wenge wood have made it a favorite with designers.**

equivalent might be African wenge wood, currently the height of fashion, dark and heavy with a straight grain and coarse texture. However, unlike the dalbergia, wenge is being replanted.

Fortunately for those who love wood as much as they love trees, the drive for sustainable lumber, harvested from properly managed forests, has led to new standards, making it possible to make sure the new wood we purchase is genuinely "environmentally friendly." There is now a globally recognized environmental standard for wood, which has been put forward by the international Forest Stewardship Council. Any wood bearing the FSC logo can be bought with a clear conscience.

Buying hardwoods, such as oak, sycamore, ash, beech, elm, and cherry, from countries that have signed up to these new international standards stimulates a market for the more valuable and expensive woods, giving woodland owners a financial incentive to husband their stock of trees. The majority of the world's farmed trees are still used to provide cheap fuel and paper. These softwood plantation trees can sell for as little as a few dollars each. Hardwoods, used for more high-value products such as furniture, are comparatively expensive. A single hardwood log from an old tree with a desirable color and grain may fetch several thousand dollars.

ABOVE, ABOVE LEFT, AND LEFT: In contemporary interiors, a material used by man since ancient times looks modern and sassy. The dark good looks of wenge wood (above left), used here for bathroom cabinets, have made it a favorite with designers. Chengal wooden treads are mounted on a metal spine (left) for a sculptural staircase in Singapore. Like chunky Venetian blinds, these slatted wooden doors filter light (above).

THIS PAGE: Comfortable dining depends on a combination of factors, as any successful restaurateur will tell you; the support and comfort of a chair, the height of a table, the quality of light. The combination of custom-made oak table and the wide, high-backed Jean-Michel Frank wooden chairs with their smooth covering of woven cane looks particularly inviting in this house in Belgium. The narrow planking of the table attractively echoes the bleached teak planks of the floor.

ABOVE: Wooden plates, the forerunners of china, still have a tactile appeal, despite the inconvenience of not being dishwasher-proof. Wooden-handled flatware feels good in the hand—warm and smooth. And, unlike china, metal, and glass, wood is quiet, its sounds muted compared with the clatter of harder materials. Seated at this oak table (above), settled on a Hans Wegner "Wishbone" chair, with a wooden plate ready to be filled, you could be sure of a meal as aurally soothing as visually appealing.

The distinction between hard- and softwoods is a commercial one and is not wholly accurate as a purely descriptive term. Trees that produce softwoods are conifers, evergreens with tough needlelike leaves. These are the most ancient species of tree, including giant redwood trees, which were found in the Jurassic period, 195 million years ago. Spruces, pines, and fir trees are the most commonly cultivated sources of softwoods, generally growing faster than their deciduous cousins, giving a loosely grained, relatively light wood that is easy to cut, shape, and stain. However, a 150-year-old Douglas fir will yield a much harder, rot-resistant wood than a young yellow pine, while yew trees, which can live for more than a thousand years, provide a wood so strong it was the fabric for the lethal English longbow.

Hardwoods are the lumber of broad-leaved trees and range from the extremely hard, such as ebony, to a wood such as beech, which will quickly deteriorate when exposed to the weather.

RIGHT AND FAR RIGHT:
Different woods have been used for interior detailing in this house in Idaho, from paneled doors in pale oak (right) to a birch staircase and baseboard (far right).
BELOW: Traditional rush seating, perfectly in harmony with its bent oak frame, has been "soaped" for a smooth, matt finish.

While a softwood tree may be ready to be felled after forty years of growth, an oak would not be mature enough until it had been growing for at least a century. This slower rate of growth contributes to the denser structure of hardwoods, the fibrous components of which consist of long narrow cells with thick walls. These walls are impregnated with lignin, which remains after the cells have died and which keeps the cell shape rigid.

After felling and cutting at the sawmill, lumber that is to be used for construction or furniture must be seasoned, dried, and hardened to minimize movement. Freshly cut wood is thick with sap and moisture. Today's commercial wood is kiln-dried. In past centuries lumber was air-dried and left stacked under cover, sometimes for years, before it was ready to be worked.

Even the most thoroughly seasoned lumber continues to move slightly in reaction to atmospheric conditions, expanding with an increase in moisture, contracting as it dries out. Various methods of minimizing warping have been devised over the centuries. Plywood, which sandwiches three or more thin layers of wood together with the grain running crosswise, has been used since the eighteenth century and was particularly popular with the nineteenth-century Biedermeier craftsmen of Austria and Germany long before modernists such as Alvar Aalto and Marcel Breuer made it their own. Pianos, from the late ninteenth century on, were always made from laminated wood, which partly explains their disproportionate weightiness. The solution for today's carpenters has been medium-density fiberboard, made by binding the waste fibers of wood that are a byproduct of processing at the sawmill with glues for a heavy, dense board with a fine surface suitable for painting.

For some purposes, unseasoned "green" wood is chosen. Traditional wooden frame buildings which use mortise and tenon joints, secured with wooden pegs, make structural allowance for gradual shrinkage. While wood that has been nailed will split if it expands or contracts too much, a mortise, or notch, with a tenon, or tongue of wood slotted into it, anchored with a piece of wooden dowel, will move in unison without putting any extra strain on the point of joining.

Softwoods have traditionally been used for woodwork that was painted, or for kitchen furniture. Pine was the wood most commonly used for interiors. Being cheap and plentiful, it was a low-status wood, only fit for servants or disguise. Stripped pine—often marketed as part of the period-living package—was a late twentieth-century fashion that would have been anathema to our European ancestors. Pine paneling, doors, shutters, and window frames were always painted, sometimes grained to look

OPPOSITE PAGE AND ABOVE: The cupboard-lined space between bedroom and bathroom in this London apartment owes its atmosphere of luxury to the richness of its materials; polished parquet in African muhuhu wood and sapele pomelle, a veneer cut from another African hardwood tree, banded with dark iroko, for cupboards and paneling. Handles and light switches are bronze, and the lampshade (above) is vellum.

> **"Softwoods have traditionally been used for wood that was painted."**

like a more expensive wood. Even pine kitchen hutches were usually painted. Only the kitchen tabletop was left naked so it could be bleached and scrubbed.

Hardwoods, especially those imported from exotic climes, were the raw material of the fine cabinetmaker: mahogany, with its rich coloring; rosewood with its prominent, wavering grain; dramatic Virginia walnut. The patterns of grain were matched and maximized, and intricate marquetries and inlays exploited different colors of wood to create designs of remarkable variety.

During the second half of the nineteenth century in Britain, the Arts and Crafts movement, with William Morris at its head, championed a return to the use of indigenous woods for furniture, "honestly" constructed and simple in design. Oak became their chosen medium, harking back to the Middle Ages when it was the wood most often used for fine furniture.

At the beginning of a new century, following a period that has seen the appearance of more new materials for household furnishings than any previous, from plastic to chrome, Formica to brushed steel, wood in its plain, "honest" guise is again in fashion. And, although we cannot congratulate ourselves on being the first generation to legislate for the protection of trees, (an act as early as 1581 attempted to control the destruction of English oak forests and the seventeenth-century diarist John Evelyn campaigned for the replanting of woodland) as long as we choose carefully, we can enjoy wood without feeling guilty.

THIS PAGE AND OPPOSITE: Some wooden artefacts seem far removed from their origins—carved, inlaid, polished, stained, and lacquered to a point where it is impossible to imagine they ever belonged to a tree. This undulating teak chair from Japan (opposite) is at the other extreme—a piece of furniture so reminiscent of its leafy parent it could almost be rooted in the rug. Battered woven cane suitcases—made from ribs of split rattan, a type of Malaysian palm tree— show wood in yet another of its many incarnations (above left). A chaste cedarwood box and heavy bookend (bottom far left) leave the grain of the wood to speak for itself.

THIS PAGE AND OPPOSITE:
Since the Hanging Gardens
of Babylon, with its tree-lined
terraces irrigated by a
reservoir at its summit, stone
and water have been
combined with plants to
create some of the world's
most ravishing gardens. Two
gardens in Singapore use this
ancient partnership to make
outdoor spaces that are as
modern as they are serene.
Water spills from the corner of
a stone block that projects
from a rusticated block wall
(opposite) and trickles down
an angled slope of travertine
into a dark pool (left).

stone

At once commonplace and remarkable, stone is the most ancient material we are ever likely to handle. Quarried and mined, stone has been used for thousands of years for shelters and tools, for sculptures and tombs, for paving, cobbles, mosaics, and even furniture. Cooked in the bowels of the earth, or compressed from sediments laid down over millions of years, there are hundreds of different types of stone, each showing an infinite variety of texture, color, and pattern.

Stone is possessed of qualities that, over the centuries, have given it a unique cultural significance. The stuff of cliffs, mountains, and caves, stone represents shelter, strength, permanence, and solidity. Castles are built of stone and so are the firmest foundations. But there is also a more mysterious, otherworldly quality to this substance that shapes our landscape.

Peoples of every culture have set up stones for religious purposes, especially stones of meteoric origin that were once believed to have fallen to earth from heaven itself. Local superstitions invariably pertain to prominent or bizarre rock formations—especially those with anthropomorphic or zoomorphic attributes. These stones are often thought to be endowed with magic powers. Even stones as small as pebbles have been accorded supernatural abilities. Flints with natural holes worn through them, known as "hag stones," were once strung up on front doors, hung around the neck or on bedposts to guard against witches, the evil eye, and nightmares.

Stones and rocks figure large in myth and legend. Scylla and Charybdis were said to inhabit rocks on the coast of Sicily, while some of the most terrible and terrifying witches and monsters have used their powers to turn the living to stone. Excalibur lay embedded in a stone that would release its grip on the sword's blade only in response to the touch of the future King of England, King Arthur. The Pied Piper led the children of Hamelin to a rocky mountain cave where they all disappeared, save two, while the command "Open Sesame!" gained entrance to the robbers' rocky cave in the tale of the Forty Thieves.

Stone fascinates us partly because it seems to combine organic qualities—its infinite variety, its patterning of veins and fossil remains—with qualities that are anathema to life. Stone dead, stone cold,

rock hard all allude to the adamantine nature of rock and stone—its harsher, inhuman side. Conversely, whether marble chiseled silken smooth by Michelangelo, or a beach pebble rolled and rubbed by waves, stone can be worked, worn, and polished for a surface as velvety as skin. Considering the extraordinary and ancient history of even the most humble pebble, it is hardly surprising if we have sometimes aggrandized stone with mysterious powers, while at the same time appreciating its strengths as a building material of beauty and longevity.

The oldest known rocks are at least 3.9 billion years old, which is almost as old as the earth itself. All rocks contain crystals of naturally occurring elements called minerals, of which there are more than a thousand found on earth. Some rocks only contain one mineral, others are combinations of six or more. The different, often extreme, conditions under which these minerals have combined give us the three main types of rock known as igneous, sedimentary, and metamorphic. Over millions

THIS PAGE AND OPPOSITE: A pervading sense of calm and unity has been achieved by the architects of this contemporary house in Belgium, where polished limestone covers floors and stairs (below left). In the bathroom, the same stone lines the walls, wraps the bathtub and serves as shelving. The choice of a warm brown mussel limestone, mottled with fossil remains, means the effect is neither sterile nor uniform. A simple, ridged detailing provides contrast of texture.

and millions of years, these three types of rock have been engaged in an unimaginably slow but continuous rearrangement of the earth's crust—a process that persists every moment of every day in a cycle of endless combustion, erosion, and compression.

Almost 90 per cent of the earth's crust is made from igneous rock. This type of rock is formed when molten magma from the earth's fiery interior cools and crystallizes. Solidified lava is igneous. Granite is also an igneous rock formed from magma, but one that has cooled much more slowly, far below ground. The larger the grains, or crystals, of granite, the slower and deeper the rock has been been created.

While the crust of the earth is mostly igneous rock, some 75 per cent of the world's land surface is covered with thin layers of debris—mud, clay, eroded fragments of rock, the remains of plants and animals—that build up and compact over millions of years to form sedimentary rocks. The character of this type of rock is determined by the nature of the debris from which it is formed. Most sandstones consist of medium-sized grains of quartz, visible to the naked eye, which have been deposited in shallow seas. Shelly limestones are made mainly from broken shells or the skeletons of sea creatures. Oolitic limestone is formed from fine sand grains or shell fragments that have been coated in the soluble mineral calcite.

The ground floor of this converted warehouse, where fashion designer Johanne Riss lives and works, is a showroom, living room, and yard in one. Lit by a huge window, the room is floored in stone and concrete, and is partially occupied by a pond and shaded by giant pot plants. A boulder incorporated into the pond wall contributes to the mix of indoor furnishing and outdoor features.

The last group of rocks are the metamorphic rocks, which include marble and slate. As their name suggests, these are rocks that have been changed from other types of rock, either as a result of baking due to their proximity to molten magma, or squeezing by the movements of vast tectonic plates. Marble metamorphoses from limestone when intense heat or pressure recrystallizes the calcite that it contains. Pure limestones are transformed into white marble that sparkles like icing, while muddier limestones may have veins or patches caused by the crystallization of other minerals they contain. Slate forms when a shale or mudstone is subjected to such pressure that its mineral content is realigned into smooth, flat layers.

Because of the difficulty and expense of transporting stone, indigenous architecture has historically been characterized by the nature of local building materials. Scottish architecture is dominated by granite—giving Aberdeen its nickname, "Granite City." The Cotswolds are characterized by a warm, golden limestone, also used for roof tiles, where it weathers from yellow to gray to black as it reacts with the acid in rainwater, the resulting silt providing ample food for lichen. Sandstone was used to rebuild London after the Great Fire of 1666. New York's "brownstone" townhouses are constructed from pinky-brownish sandstone.

The hefty exposed stone chimney breast, rugged and rural, is an American vernacular dating back to a pioneering past when farmers built their own log cabins, limiting the more difficult work of cutting and laying local stone to the one part of the structure where it was most needed. These contemporary houses in the Idaho mountains by architect Mark Pynn use indoor stone symbolically and decoratively rather than as a structural necessity, for a look that is both modern, in its emphasis on the color and texture of an unprocessed natural material, and historical. In accordance with tradition, both chimney breasts use local stone. The strong horizontals of the left-hand wall are cut from Idaho quartzite, in a blend of "honeyledgestone" and "sunset gold" for a mix of gray and brown that picks up the tones of the wooden floor and cupboards. The random blocks (right) are a darker stone called "Fairfield," dry-stacked with deep-raked joints leaving their gently rounded shapes outlined in shadow.

The availability of stone profoundly affects the nature of vernacular architecture worldwide. A lavish use of marble continues to dominate Italian architecture. The terracotta pantiles of much of the Mediterranean point to a scarcity of slate. Despite the huge improvements in transportation that have occurred this century, "organic" architects in the wake of Frank Lloyd Wright and Henry van de Velde continue to argue that the use of locally available materials, when financially viable, is key to the success of integrating a new building into its surrounding landscape.

Building with stone has always been expensive. The use of stone in interiors has been limited by expense, but also practicality. Stone will never be cheap, but the range of its home applications has been revolutionized by recent advances in chemical sealants. Keeping a flagstone floor clean used to be a question of a large scrubbing brush, plenty of warm soapy water, and liberal elbow grease. Today's limestone floors, once sealed, can simply be mopped. This increased practicality has led in turn to increased demand—the U.S. being the biggest single market. Quarries all over the world have reopened, while those already in production have increased their efficiency and output. Inexpensive and decorative slates for floors, work surfaces, and shelving are now imported from India and China. Welsh slate remains the best quality and the most suitable for roofing, and this is reflected in its price. Limestone is quarried all over the world; the tiles under your feet in the most stylish hotel foyers, stores, and restaurants may have traveled all the way from the West Bank of Jerusalem, from Burgundy, from the hills of southern Valencia, from Portugal, Germany, or Mexico.

Slate can be quarried manually, requiring little in the way of sophisticated machinery. It splits easily into flat sheets due to its layered structure—a characteristic that has long been exploited for roof tiles, flooring and, indeed, billiard tables. Unless slate is being used for kitchen work surfaces, in which case it is usually polished, it is laid as "riven" along its naturally parallel cleavage planes, leaving ripples of texture over its surface.

Limestone is far more difficult to extract and requires more work before it is ready for use. Limestone must be cut into massive blocks on site. It cannot be split by hand, and sometimes a whole face of rock has to be thrown away because of a single fault line. At the factory, limestone blocks are cut into slabs using gang saws with diamond blades, the ferocious friction dampened by copious quantities of water, the precious diamonds requiring frequent replacement. After cutting, there are various finishing techniques used to achieve different effects. Sleek modern interiors tend to use pale, even-colored limestone that has been fine-sanded and polished. More rustic finishes include flame texturing and bush hammering, both of which give a less shiny and more textured look to the stone. "Tumbled" limestone has an antiqued appearance and is therefore an economical alternative to reclaimed limestone for use in an old building.

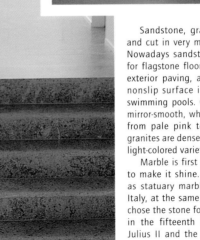

OPPOSITE PAGE: Interior designer Aude Cardinale has transformed an old factory in Paris into a home of exceptional chic. Limestone flooring in pale sand adds an architectural grandeur to spaces once devoted to the manufacture of pressure cookers.
RIGHT: A darker type of limestone (right) sweeps up the stairs and along the landing of a contemporary house in Belgium.
ABOVE RIGHT: Polished concrete blends well with redwood wall paneling and exposed brickwork in a modernist house in the Hollywood Hills.

Sandstone, granite, and marble are quarried and cut in very much the same way as limestone. Nowadays sandstone, once the traditional stone for flagstone flooring, is more frequently used for exterior paving, as its slightly rough texture and nonslip surface is ideal for terraces, paths, and swimming pools. Granite looks dull until polished mirror-smooth, when its coloring, which can range from pale pink to jet black, is revealed. Darker granites are denser, and therefore stronger, than the light-colored varieties.

Marble is first polished, then waxed and sealed to make it shine. Pure white marble, also known as statuary marble, is still quarried at Carrara in Italy, at the same quarry from which Michelangelo chose the stone for some of his greatest works back in the fifteenth century, including the tomb of Julius II and the *Pietà*. This purest, most pristine form of marble possesses a lustrous sheen and luminescent quality due to the way that light penetrates the stone and reflects from the surfaces of inner crystals, creating a sparkling effect.

There are many man-made substitutes for real stone. They include various types of reconstituted stone made from binding stone dust with resins to form a putty that can be molded before it dries to set hard. Reconstituted stone is particularly popular for garden ornaments and statues that would be prohibitively expensive carved from the real thing. There is also a wide selection of fake stone paving for outdoors, some more palatable than others. There is even vinyl flooring that looks remarkably like stone mosaic. Then there is concrete, in all its forms, from the ugly and grotesque (mock stone siding being the worst offender) to the surprisingly chic and pleasant when it is polished for interior use.

The best substitute stones achieve a good visual approximation to the material they imitate and are invariably cheaper. However, no substitute has yet been devised that ages and weathers with the grace of stone. The evidence is everywhere. Compare cobblestones with asphalt, stone paving with cement slabs, concrete steps with granite ones. Exposed to the elements, stone plays host to lichens and mosses where concrete simply stains. Stone may erode, crumble, even split, but its patina won't be lost. An old stone doorstep bows gracefully where generations of feet have worn it away, grain by grain. An old flagstone floor shines from scrubbing and treading. Marble in an entrance hall gains a deeper, richer gloss by the decade.

Real stone adds weight, both literally and metaphorically, and a sense of permanence to any interior; comfortingly solid beneath the feet, reassuringly invulnerable for work surfaces, and always beautiful. Stone remains a luxury, if an increasingly affordable one, but a luxury that will stand the test of time.

> "No substitute has yet been devised that ages and weathers with the grace of stone."

LEFT: Concrete meets limestone at the foot of a staircase in Aude Cardinale's converted factory, a meeting of the manufactured and the natural. In fact, polished concrete comes out of it rather well, its appearance more varied and organic than you would expect of a man-made, mass-produced material with a reputation for brutality. OPPOSITE PAGE: The real thing: mussel limestone covering the stairs in a Belgian house—beautiful in its uncompromising, banister-free simplicity.

ELEMENTS

38 stone

Ever since the Ice Age, half a million years ago, when prehistoric man wrapped himself against the biting wind in the pelts of the animals he ate, leather has been our second skin. Strong, supple, scented, and luxurious, modern leathers have never been more desirable or more versatile. In contemporary interiors, leather and skins are not only used for upholstery and cushions, but also in the guise of rugs and throws, bedspreads and accessories, and even floor tiles.

leather

For one of life's most sensual luxuries, leather has a pretty sordid and unappetizing past. While retaining in its finished state all the character and charm of a natural material, leather has traveled a long, soggy, and decidedly malodorous route before it stretches itself, serene and scented, over the seat of your Aston Martin or dimples into glossy buttoning on your elegant Mies van der Rohe chair.

In fact, thanks to modern methods of tanning using mineral salts, tanneries are no longer evil-smelling hellholes, shunned by the sensitive noses of polite society. Indeed, today's processes are positively fragrant compared with the practices of the past. In the eighteenth and nineteenth centuries, London tanneries employed, among other noxious substances, stagnant urine, while Henry Mayhew reported in his Victorian survey, *London Labour and the London Poor*, that some poor souls literally scraped a living collecting dog excrement from the streets for the same purpose. Little wonder, then, that Southwark, where London's tanneries were concentrated, was a no-go area characterized by its preponderance of theaters and lowlife.

Leather can be made from the skin of any animal, bird, reptile, or fish. The most commonly used leathers today are a by-product of animals reared for meat, milk, and wool, with cattle and sheep accounting for more than 80 per cent of the world's leather production. To transform a raw skin into a material that is both durable and malleable is initially a question of halting the process of decomposition. All fine leather originates in the blood-stained halls of the abattoir, where skins are salted as a temporary preservative. This is how they arrive at the tannery: "wet salted," slimy, and altogether unappealing. Washing in enormous wooden tubs removes the salt. The next wash in a solution of lime and sodium sulfide removes the hair and top layer of the skin, known as the epidermis. Once the hide has been cleaned, it may be split through its thickness, the under- or flesh side of the hide to make suede, the top grained layer a leather suitable for upholstery.

OPPOSITE PAGE: Pale mushroom-brown nubuck leather upholstery and matching pillows in Aude Cardinale's Paris living room. The soft and velvety finish that characterizes nubuck is the result of gently buffing, or sanding, the tanned cattle hide on its outer "grain" side.
ABOVE LEFT: A trio of pillows sit on Bernie de Le Cuona's sofa, two in suede, and one in silky "glove" leather. Suede can either be produced by abrasion on the grain surface of leather, like nubuck, or by buffing the split surface of a hide that has been divided, or split in two to give twice the amount of leather from a single hide.
ABOVE: A plump, welcoming "club" armchair is upholstered in smooth brown cattlehide leather.

After splitting, the hide is delimed to remove all traces of alkali, "bated" in a weak enzyme to make the grain finer and the end product smoother and more elastic, and finally "pickled" ready for tanning. Tanning is the crucial step from unstable protein to durable fabric, and the point after which the hide metamorphoses into leather. Early man probably shortcircuited the process by stretching animal skins in the sun to dry, halting decay but failing to retain any of the softness and flexibility that make leather so versatile and desirable. Centuries later, it was discovered that rubbing the brains of animals into the pores of a hide could soften it. At some yet later stage, the unique properties of tannin or tannic acid, found in the bark of certain trees or in oak galls, finally allowed the manufacture of leather much as we know it today. In those countries where oak was not available, tannic acid could be extracted from the sumac plant. Hides had to be soaked for months, even years, before they could be used, but already in Pre-Dynastic Egypt, before 5000 B.C., leather was in demand for clothing, sandals, and bottles. Egyptian mummies were often carried to burial under a pall of pale blue leather.

Most modern leathers are tanned using minerals—trivalent chromium sulfate, to be precise. First developed in the 1950s in response to the demand from the furniture industry for a softer, more flexible leather, chromium tanning salts work their magic in a matter of hours rather than months. After tanning, hides are "dressed," which means shaving them to an even thickness, and treated with emulsion oils such as natural fish oil to lubricate the fiber structure. At this stage the hides are ready to be dyed.

Modern dyes are so sophisticated that a dressed cowhide, which arrives at the tannery an indeterminate beige hue and emerges from the chrome tanning process a rather attractive shade of pale duck-egg blue, can then reemerge from a vat of dye in practically any color of the rainbow, from deep inky black to rich heavy cream. Dripping with color, the hides are now "set" to remove any creases and excess water, and are then hung up to dry naturally.

THIS PAGE AND OPPOSITE: An air of discreet and rather masculine luxury pertains to leather upholstery, reminiscent as it is of gentlemen's clubs, old libraries, smoking rooms, and expensive cars. Devoid of pattern, bar the regular irregularities of its grain (far left), smooth, glossy, and strong, leather improves with age, developing a patina like the wood it is so often matched with. In Aude Cardinale's Paris house (opposite above right), leather the color of sweet butter stretches over a pair of Art Deco-style armchairs. A cowhide rug—leather that has been dressed and finished with the hair left on—covers the floor. The remainder of the pictures show furniture from a London apartment designed by James Gorst, including armchairs in mustard and oxblood leather by Philippe Hurel and a mahogany plywood chair with a black leather seat by Sawaya and Moroni. The leather sofa (above) is by Andree Putman for De Sede.

> *"Just like a human
> fingerprint, each
> hide carries its own
> unique history."*

The last stages of this lengthy progress, from raw to ready-to-wear, are the finishing processes, a combination of coatings and treatments such as buffing, embossing, and milling that will determine the final feel and appearance of the leather. Although today's tanneries are largely mechanized, and despite the fact that modern chemicals have vastly accelerated the laborious tasks of tanning and dyeing, it still takes about twenty-three different processes and some five weeks to transform a single hide into a piece of usable leather. Throughout its journey through the factory, each hide is inspected by hand time and again. Scars and blemishes are common—scratches from a brush against barbed wire, marks of disease, brands. No two hides are ever alike. Just like a human fingerprint, each hide carries its own unique history.

A visit to a tannery can only increase one's respect for this extraordinary material, created by nature, preserved thanks to man's ingenuity. Attempts to reproduce its characteristics synthetically have never been particularly successful. Imitation suede and

ABOVE: The contrast of cool, shiny metal with leather upholstery is a cliché of modernist furniture design. Classic twentieth-century chairs like Le Corbusier's "Grand Confort" and Mies van der Rohe's Barcelona chair, all play on this disparity between modern materials and process techniques and a traditional use of leather upholstery, and all look as contemporary as the day they were first sat upon. The Charles Eames chair and ottoman above, upholstered in dark brown leather, is a fine example of a design that has lost none of its freshness, its elegant aluminum skeleton highlighted against the iroko paneling in a London apartment.

RIGHT AND OPPOSITE: Also by Charles Eames is this screen in undulating panels of ash plywood, which sits in a house in the Hollywood Hills (right) renovated by architect Stephen Slan. Undulating in a different direction is the "Listen to Me" chaise by Edward Wormley, which has been reupholstered in "Superkidskin," a fine, creamy leather, deliciously soft and seductively impractical.

BELOW AND RIGHT: Leather can be made from the skin of any mammal, reptile, bird, or fish. This Art Deco dining table and sideboard in designer Aude Cardinale's house in Paris are covered in an exotic patchwork of squares of sharkskin, the color rippling through shades of stone, the texture slightly rough to the touch but eminently strokable. Known as shagreen, this type of leather has been used since the seventeenth century, most commonly for covering small boxes and tea caddies. After tanning, the finely granulated skin is ground flat so the protruding papillae make a pattern of tiny raised dots. Today the use of skins that are not a by-product of animals reared for meat, milk, and wool is strictly controlled, with 63 per cent of all leather produced being cattlehide.

OPPOSITE PAGE: In the same Paris house, a ponyskin game-board on a suede-covered table makes a game of checkers an unusually tactile business. The chairs' appearance is due to paint, not nature.

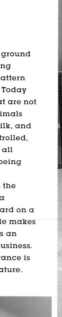

leather, however superficially convincing, always betray their ersatz nature over time. Real leather wears, rubs, and scuffs with grace. A leather coat molds itself to the body after a few weeks of wear until it feels like an old friend. A much-used leather chair becomes ever more comfortable for exactly the same reason. Leather shoes, leather bags, leather floor tiles; all seem to welcome the touch of hands and feet.

The structure of leather is a marvel of complexity, a matted web of millions of tiny stringlike fibrils, each one finer than a hair, which lies between the outer skin, with its follicles, fat glands, and erector muscles, and the layer of flesh that it has served to protect. One of the many benefits of this structure is that it contains a great deal of air, which is why leather has such excellent thermal properties—cool in summer and warm in winter. The unique structure of leather is also the secret of its elasticity and strength. Even the finest leathers are difficult to pierce, while thick hides, especially when laminated, are tough enough to have been used for shields and armor, and will stand the wear and tear of many hundreds of miles of walking when used for the sole of a shoe. Like our own skin, and unlike plastic substitutes, leather breathes.

Leather can be processed in different ways in order to adapt its qualities for different uses, but there is also a more fundamental choice between different types of hide and skin, each of which have their own peculiar properties. Ox hide is the thickest and most resilient of all, and is the leather used to make footballs. Calf, kid, and cattle hides tend to be used for shoe uppers, handbags, and wallets, while sheepskin is usually chosen for shoe linings, rugs, and book bindings. Saddles, suitcases, and fancy leather goods are likely to be pigskin, while snake, crocodile, alligator, and lizard skins are the preserve of expensive handbags and shoes. Upholstery is almost always made from cowhide, which combines softness and

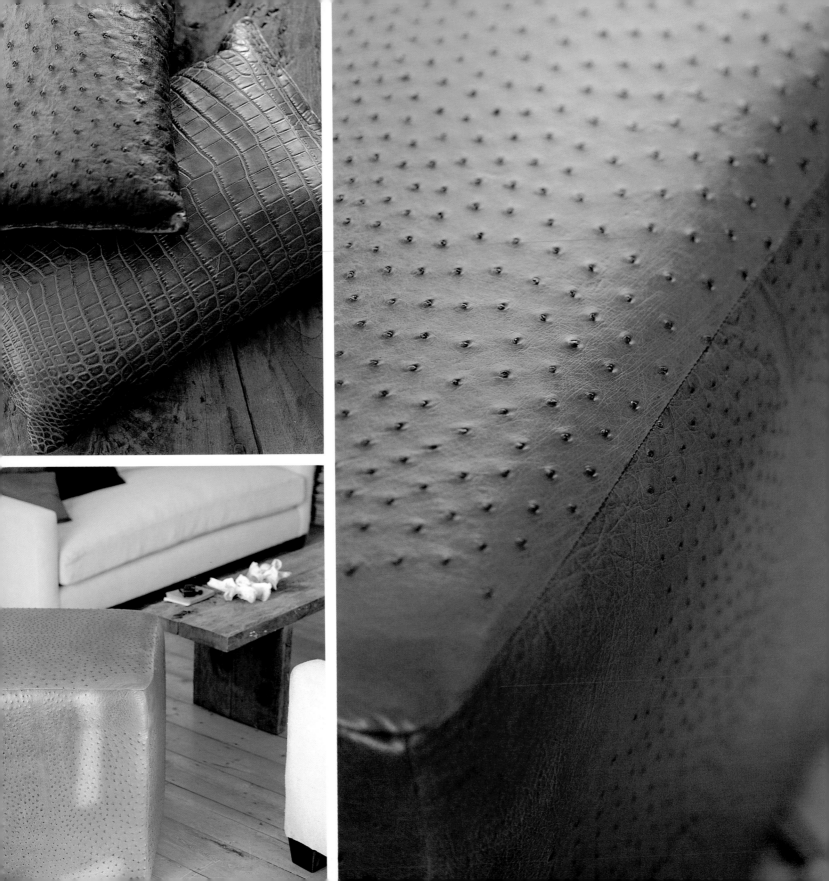

culturally taboo, in France there are butchers who specialize in horse meat, and goat is a delicacy in many African countries. Cultural scruples are likely to dissolve when face to face, or hand to hair, with one of these furry hides, and they are increasingly sought both as floor coverings and upholstery.

The appeal of fur, or hair and wool as these skins should more correctly be referred to, seems as primal as our attraction toward the bright warmth of a fire or the burble of running water. The most popular pets have long been those with the softest, most strokable fur. When we bury our fingers in the curly neck of a golden retriever or brush a hand down a cat's back, the pleasure is entirely reciprocal. Grooming our own hair is something of an obsession. Children play affectionately with each other's hair in exactly the same way that chimpanzees indulge in social grooming. As adults, we pay for the services of a hairdresser to do the same. Resisting the urge to fondle a sheepskin is in the same category of extreme difficulty as eating a sugary jelly doughnut without licking your lips.

Just as leather carries with it some of the unique characteristics of the animal from which it originated, so no two sheepskins will ever be exactly the same. More obvious are the differences in age and origin of the animals from which the skins have been taken. Sheepskins from Spanish Merino lambs combine the silkiest suede with a pile as

resilience. Because the average adult cowhide varies from between 45 and 200 square feet, sufficiently large pieces can be cut to avoid too many seams. Even so, it takes at least eight cowhides to cover a sofa and two armchairs.

Leather has many practical advantages that cannot be exactly reproduced, but the reasons we choose it for the interiors of our finest cars instead of velour, or to upholster a sofa instead of vinyl, run deeper than a straightforward desire for good performance. The feel and smell of real leather are as impossible to imitate as they are difficult to describe. There is a strong element of the animal in both—a faint whiff of clean puppy and trampled straw, a texture that is as soft and resilient as human skin. This is the sensual attraction of leather, the pull that makes you want to run a hand along the backbone of a leather sofa, or hold a suede pillow against your cheek.

If leather is a sensual siren, animal skins that retain their hair are sensual magnets. Distinct from furs such as fox, mink, and wolf, which most people prefer to experience as synthetic fakes, sheepskin, goatskin, cowskin, and ponyskin rugs are, like leather, by-products of the food industry. While in the U. S. and Britain, pony and goat meat are

THIS PAGE AND OPPOSITE:
Different types of leather in Bernie de Le Cuona's living room provide an array of organic texture. The cube (left and opposite below) and top pillow (opposite above) are ostrich leather, its patterning the legacy of the bird's magnificent plumage. Ostrich is farmed for its meat, but its leather is a fashionable by-product. Crocodile is also farmed for its meat and skin. Old suitcases in crocodile skin (above) show a patina of age yet to be acquired by the new crocodile pillow (opposite above). A butter-soft leather pillow (right) has been perforated for added textural interest.

OPPOSITE PAGE: The fireside rug must be one of the oldest comforts known to man. This Mongolian sheepskin in Bernie de Le Cuona's kitchen and living room is irresistibly soft, promising to bury bare toes and cushion tired limbs where the warmth and flicker of the fire already act as a magnet. The extreme contrast between the stone flags and the abundant curls of the rug adds to an appreciation of both.
LEFT AND INSET RIGHT: Leather and suede cushions and a fringed suede throw on the sofa. The leather handbag is a reminder of a more common use for this versatile material.

downy as cashmere. Icelandic sheepskins have thick, luxuriant wool, shag-pile deep. Mongolian lambskins rejoice in little corkscrew curls. These are rugs for the bedside and fireside, to cushion bare feet and envelop the toes.

Ponyskin, cowskin, goatskin, and the rare zebra skins that may come onto the market as the result of necessary culls have a more subtle tactile appeal as well as the attraction of natural markings. The stripes that wrap the body of a zebra take on the beauty of an abstract painting when laid flat over a floor. Natural cowskins retain the distinctive asymmetrical markings of the animal—random ink-blots of black and white from Friesians, coffee and cream from Normandy cows.

Unlike wool, which has no obvious nap, the hair on these skins changes direction, sweeping from the center in waves, curling into whirlpools, guiding a stroking hand in particular directions. Despite all the processes of curing and tanning, a ponyskin, for example, feels just as sleek and silken as a thoroughbred's neck. These shorter-haired skins, once the preserve of the fashion industry, are now being used for upholstery as an alternative to leather, as well as for rugs.

Every year some 15,000 million square feet of leather rolls out of the world's tanneries. Most of it, about 60 per cent, will be turned into shoes, a further 16 per cent will make clothing and accessories, while a mere 9 per cent will cover chairs, sofas, and the seats of cars and airplanes. Modern processing methods continue to improve on nature's work, so contemporary leathers are stain-, light- and moisture-resistant as never before. Always desirable, leather is becoming ever more practical for use in the home. Meanwhile, designers are responding by using this venerable material in new and imaginative ways.

natural fabrics

A time-traveler from a hundred years ago visiting any one of us today would be utterly baffled by the gadgets and home appliances, the switches and buttons, that facilitate our daily lives. But amid all this progress and built-in obsolescence, there are some threads of consistency that have lasted for hundreds, even thousands, of years. Tutankhamun's handwoven linen shirt is a garment whose fabric would be just as familiar and desirable for a shirt, dress, curtain, or pillow cover today.

Linens, cottons, wools, and silks—these natural fabrics were all well-known to our ancestors, and their appearance and feel have changed relatively little over the centuries. What has changed dramatically is their availability and their cost. Prior to the spate of inventions toward the end of the eighteenth century that gave birth to the Industrial Revolution and its dark, satanic mills, the spinning and weaving of wool and flax were cottage industries. Spinning, with a distaff and spindle, was considered womens' work—hence the term "spinster"—and was a major home occupation for all but the very wealthy. Silks and cottons had to be imported to Europe and America; silks from the Far East, cottons from India.

It is hard for us to imagine today how precious and extortionately expensive these natural textiles once were. Preindustrial methods of producing any fabric were highly labor-intensive and time-consuming. When Mary Queen of Scots used a cope, chasuble, and four tunicles to make bed hangings for Darnley, she was neither being mean nor irreverent. Fine fabrics were endlessly recycled

Today's man-made fibers can do extraordinary things: react to light and moisture, resist wrinkles and stains, incorporate fiber optics. Yet, despite the triumphs of modern technology, still we turn back to nature. Our love affair with linen, wool, cotton, and silk continues uninterrupted by chemistry and its woven wonders. Natural fibers have also found their way onto our floors as matting derived from all manner of plants, from banana leaves to a species of Chinese grass.

even in the grandest households, dresses were altered to keep up with the latest fashions, stockings darned, sheets patched. Case-covers of less expensive materials such as linen were used to protect more expensive damask and velvet on beds and chairs. More than a means of making pretty patterns, patchwork was just another way to make sure even the most thread-bare garments could be reused.

Silk was first used for textiles at a very early period in China, where the mulberry silk moth, the *Bombyx mori*, was indigenous; the oldest surviving fragments of Chinese silk date from around 1000 B.C. According to legend, the art of sericulture was discovered by a Chinese sage-queen called Lei Zu. Drinking her tea one day, she accidentally dropped a silkworm cocoon into her cup. When she pulled it out, the hot liquid had dissolved the cocoon into a mass of long, smooth strands. The secrets of sericulture were closely guarded for centuries by the Chinese, who treated its production with such reverence that loud voices and talk of death were strictly forbidden in the presence of the precious cocoons. Silk was much prized by the Romans, who regularly used it to pay taxes, and was the treasure chosen to ransom Rome from the Goths. Centuries later, Medieval monks risked their lives smuggling silkworms along the Silk Road from Asia to Europe, hiding them in the folds of their sleeves or the hollows of their staves.

Although the preparatory and weaving processes of silk production are now largely mechanized, the processes by which thousands of

THIS PAGE AND OPPOSITE: This pillow cover is made from an antique French grain sack. The rough texture of the coarse linen is much appreciated by Roger Oates' and Fay Morgan's Jack Russell terrier. In the same house (opposite below right), an antique French linen sheet of a finer weave drapes the sofa, and modern linen covers pillows (opposite below left). The stair runner (opposite above left) is a wool pile carpet, and the floor runner is "Venetian" flatweave wool. The curtains (opposite above right) are hung flat so folds do not disrupt the pattern.

yards of yarn are obtained from a fluffy cocoon still begin with a swift plunge into boiling water. This brutal bath kills the metamorphosing caterpillar and melts some of the gum that has glued the filaments together. Once separated, the filaments are graded; finer threads come from the inner layer of the cocoon, rougher ones from the surface layers. Once dried, the threads can be twisted into yarn. Raw silk, which is spun from broken filaments and damaged cocoons, is cleaned, carded, and dressed by machine in much the same way as flax or wool. This "slubby" type of silk is particularly fashionable for interiors, due to its pleasing texture and luster. Wild silk, collected by tribal Indians from mulberry trees growing naturally in the Indian jungle, also has a more knobbly feel than cultivated silks.

The relative price of silk has plummeted in the last few decades, to the extent that a pure silk shirt is now often no more expensive than its cotton equivalent. Linen, on the other hand, once the fabric of all underwear and sheets, has gained a luxury status partly due to the fact that to be experienced at its best it requires such careful laundering.

Before the nineteenth century, when cotton became widely available, linen was used not only for tablecloths and napkins, but also for sheets, pillowcases, towels, and undergarments. Always highly regarded for its coolness of touch and exceptional absorbency, linen was particularly valued by our ancestors for its ability to stand up to frequent washing. Even in Tudor times, not a period we immediately associate with high standards of personal hygiene, everyone, whether rich or poor, wore a linen undergarment, the idea being that everything that touched your skin should be washable. Anyone who could manage it would have a clean undershirt every day, while the wealthy, who had plentiful supplies of linen and plentiful servants to launder it, might change several times a day.

Linen was first grown in Egypt. During the Middle Ages, fields of blue flowering flax became common in the Low Countries and Ireland, where it thrived in the damp soil. After harvesting, the

THIS PAGE AND OPPOSITE: Belgian fashion designer Johanne Riss has used hundreds of yards of white cotton in her converted banana warehouse, which doubles as showroom, offices, and a home for herself and her two grown-up children. White cotton curtains act as informal and temporary room dividers, and white cotton slipcovers shroud every chair— inexpensive, washable, and a simple decorative ploy in order to achieve the sense of space and serenity that she finds vital for creativity.

stalks were tied in bundles and submerged in dammed rivers and pools for up to three weeks to separate the fibers from the rest of the plant. Nowadays most flax is "retted" in special tanks, where temperatures are carefully controlled to speed up the decomposition of the woody matter and cellular tissue that surrounds the fibers.

The next stage in the process is called "scutching"; the process of breaking the flax by passing it through fluted rollers and then beating it to remove the unwanted straw. The resulting tangled bundles are now combed or "hackled" to remove any remaining straw and make the fibers lie parallel so they can be spun into yarn. Until the mid-nineteenth century, linen was handwoven as, lacking the elasticity of wool and cotton, it was inclined to break under the strain of a power-operated loom. By the time a machine had been invented to weave linen, it had been largely replaced by cheaper cotton.

Once woven into cloth, linen undergoes several more processes, and it is these finishing techniques that largely account for variations in its quality and feel. Unbleached linen retains a pale brownish coloring, acceptable, even fashionable today, but considered highly undesirable by our ancestors, for whom the whiteness of linen was a mark of wealth and distinction. Bleaching was once a lengthy business: first the cloth was boiled in lye, a substance containing various alkalis varying from wood ash to lime, then it was laid out on the bleach greens, exposing it to air, sun, and dew and speeding the effect of the lye. Watchtowers were erected around the bleach greens to prevent theft of the linen as it lay exposed to the elements. Finally the linen was soaked in a weak solution of acids and rinsed in water. A good beating with beechwood hammers gave the cloth its smooth, glossy sheen.

Today all these processes are controlled by computers. A complicated design for weaving on a Jacquard loom can now be created and woven in days rather than weeks and months. So it may seem a little perverse that our tastes should have swung from the formality of fine, weighty, linen damasks to the more informal look of simpler weaves, unbleached cloth, and coarser yarns. For bedlinen, however, the whiter and finer remains the better—if only someone could find a way fully to mechanize the daily washing, starching, and bedmaking required to sustain the luxury.

Until the late eighteenth century, cotton was rare and linen common—a relationship that was only reversed by industrialization. Throughout the seventeenth and eighteenth centuries, cotton was regarded as an unacceptable threat to the wool and silk industries in England and France, and was variously taxed and legislated against. In England, for example, it was illegal from 1720 to 1774 to use pure cotton for dress or household purposes, though a fabric with a linen warp and cotton weft was permitted.

Cotton is woven from the fluffy fibers that surround the seeds of the cotton plant (*Gossypium*). The fruit will only ripen and produce these fibers if it enjoys two hundred days free from frost coupled with moderate rainfall and bright sunshine. It was first cultivated in India in about 1000 B.C., and subsequently in Egypt and the Mediterranean, and by the early nineteenth century America was the world's major producer. A growing population of imported slaves were used in the planting and picking until Emancipation.

Although not as strong once woven or as absorbent as linen, cotton was similarly soft and washable. But its most desirable quality was its receptiveness to printed pattern. Block-, plate-, and roller-printed cottons were highly fashionable throughout the second half of the eighteenth century and well into the nineteenth century, when their new availability brought affordable design within the reach of more people than ever.

The cotton industry in Britain grew up in Lancashire, where Victorian cotton mills employed huge numbers of men, women, and children who worked for long hours and low pay in conditions that were both noisy and dangerous. "Cotton king" mill owners became millionaires, and Manchester was nicknamed "Cottonopolis" as the center of manufacture for Britain's largest single export. Printed cottons have never fallen out of fashion since, although today's tastes tend toward more simple and understated designs or plain fabrics woven for textural interest, such as waffle-weave cotton or herringbone. Sheer, translucent cottons are also popular, and some of the finest organzas, voiles and gauzes still come from India, where the cotton industry was born.

LEFT: Voile veils the windows in a room that exclusively features cotton and linen. The difference in feel between synthetic nets and fresh cotton voile is like the difference between margarine and butter—worth paying for.

In the centuries before Britain grew rich on cotton, wool was a major export. The woolsack, a large pillow stuffed with wool, still remains the official seat of the Lord Chancellor as speaker of the House of Lords, a custom that was introduced by Edward III as a symbol of his country's staple trade. By the Middle Ages, England had emerged as the world's most important exporter of fine wool, although it was the Romans who had originally improved the quality of fleeces by selective breeding methods and who introduced the practice of shearing sheep as opposed to plucking the wool from them.

Although you might imagine that the steps from fleece to fabric would be less complex than those from cocoon or stalk to yarn, but in fact wool production is far from simple. Once sheared, wool must be graded according to texture, and is then washed, dried, loosened, and oiled before being carded or combed. Carded wool, which was originally teased out with the head of a thistle, then between the wire teeth of coarse brushes, produces a spongy mass of crisscross threads that are very soft when spun into yarn. Combing wool separates it into the long fibers only and results in a tighter, more even yarn, known as worsted.

After weaving, woolen cloth may be "fulled" in order to felt and thicken it. Until machines and more acceptable chemicals took over, this process was achieved by trampling the cloth in a solution of urine before it was washed, beaten, brushed, and finally cropped to an even surface. Despite competition from many woollike synthetics, pure wool remains most desirable for carpeting and upholstery fabrics as well as for clothes. Felt, which is produced by matting rather than weaving woolen fibers, has recently graduated from the school craft table to the stylish interior. Thick, springy, felted wools are now being used as flooring and for accessories such as cushions, bags, and book covers.

Other types of softer and even more luxurious wools have also begun to make their appearance in the home. Cashmere, woven from the fleece of Kashmir goats, was once reserved exclusively for the most fine and expensive clothes. Softer and lighter than wool, cashmere is correspondingly more delicate and so, unlike wool, is not suitable for upholstery. However, the passion for luxurious texture in our homes, which has accompanied the trend toward a more pared-down look, has brought cashmere out of the closet and onto the sofa. Woven and knitted cashmere pillows and generous throws are the ultimate covetable luxury for the indulgent minimalist. Pashmina shawls, fine and light as feathers, traditionally woven only for royalty using a mix of Tibetan goat wool and silk, may no longer be the height of fashion for shoulders, but have instead become chic accessories for beds and armchairs.

Wall-to-wall carpet, especially of the brightly colored and patterned variety, has suffered a loss of popularity in recent years. Although warm and yielding underfoot and, thanks to powerful vacuum cleaners, rather easier to maintain than combinations of hard flooring and rugs, brightly colored wall-to-wall pile can look out of place in an interior where natural materials and colors are the predominant decorative motif. In rooms such as childrens' bedrooms, where the warmth, comfort, and safety of carpet is most desirable, neutral, natural shades of wool carpeting look suitably unartificial.

Between the extremes of bare boards and wall-to-wall wool are the many kinds of flooring woven from vegetable fibers, which can either be fitted or laid as rugs. Some of these may be dyed or bleached for a variety of colors, but mainly they are

ABOVE: A sheepskin rug has been shorn to the curly velvet of a lamb, giving it the appearance of tufted carpet. Wool carpeting is naturally antistatic, just one of its many advantages over synthetic substitutes.

sold on the strength of their natural coloring and their textural interest, which is both a function of weave and raw material. One of the softest of these natural floorings is jute. Like a tougher version of flax, jute fibers are made from the fibrous inner bark of a large herbaceous plant that grows in hot, damp regions of Asia. Harvested by hand, the stalks are softened in water before being dried in the sun and then spun. Tougher than jute, but more susceptible to stains, is sisal, which is woven from fibers extracted from the spiky leaves of a bush grown in the subtropical regions of Brazil, Mexico, and East Africa. The toughest of all is coir, traditionally used for rope making and doormats. Coarse and prickly, coir fibers are removed from coconut husks after softening in salt water, and are then pounded by stone, combed out, and dried before weaving.

Probably the most tactile of all the natural floorings is sea-grass, which also benefits from a particularly delicious smell like freshly cut hay. Sea-grass grows in China in paddy fields that are regularly flooded by seawater. Even when the grass is harvested, dried, and spun, the resulting yarn remains surprisingly waterproof. For this reason, sea-grass cannot be dyed and is naturally stain-resistant. Combinations of wool and sisal, wool and jute, sea-grass and sisal, and even woven paper

LEFT: Fabrics are one of the most obvious ways to introduce a variety of textures into an interior in varying degrees of softness. Bernie de Le Cuona's living room mixes leather and suede pillows with linen upholstery and a silk throw. The staircase is cushioned and quietened with a carpet of hardwearing coir in a shade of golden brown that is very close to the color of the wooden floor.

and sisal continue to broaden the choice of natural floorings. Abaca, derived from banana leaves, is another newcomer to the home market. As our appetite for "honest" materials grows, ancient skills are being combined with modern manufacturing processes to produce fabrics and flooring that combine the unique appeal of the handcrafted with lower costs and availability.

Knowing that your linen pillowcase started life as a stalk or that the fibers of your matting once coated a coconut shell can only add to their appeal. Both are examples of natural structures that cannot be bettered synthetically, and instances of man's extraordinary ability to cultivate, process, and adapt the world's raw materials for his own use and pleasure.

LEFT, INSET LEFT, AND ABOVE:
Fabrics offer comfort and
relaxation. A wool rug offers an
island of warmth in the sea of
limestone flooring in a London
apartment (far left), walled in
by an L-shaped sofa. The sofas
and armchairs in this Belgian
house (above) were designed
by antique-dealer-turned-
designer Axel Vervoordt and
covered in stone-colored linen.
A workout for sensitive soles
in a stone-floored house in
Singapore (left).

natural fabrics **61**

THIS PAGE AND OPPOSITE:
Mary Shaw's elegant Paris
salon is a tribute to her
native Ireland, reflecting
the colors of its landscape,
which she describes as
"amber, plum and mossy
greens," and showcasing
its traditional textiles:
tweed and linen. Her
company, Sequana, sells
lighting, furniture, and
fabrics, and this room, as
well as home, serves as a
showroom for its products.
The mix of antiques and
contemporary pieces
designed by Mary Shaw
gives the room bite, but it
is the textiles that shape its
character—wool tweeds
and plaids, linens, blankets,
and mohair throws, all
woven in Donegal. And,
although Mary Shaw's
habit of covering chairs
and sofas in fabrics more
frequently used for suits
might appear innovative,
she is following a custom
she remembers from her
childhood in County Down,
when it was taken for
granted that the armchairs
were always covered in
local tweed and lightened
up for the summer with
linen slipcovers.

rooms

There are three powerful and often opposing forces at work when we plan a room of our own: the demands of comfort; the demands of practicality; and the tug of style. The successful resolution of all three defines a perfect room, but it is far harder to achieve than you might imagine.

The decoration of a living room forces us to face all these issues at once. Unlike bedrooms, which are private domains, or bathrooms and kitchens, where function dictates a basic level of practicality, living rooms are the space through which we can express something about ourselves to other people. Style is at a premium, on show, for all to see. This is the room, above all others, that sets the scene for our lives and tells our story to an audience.

Whatever interior decorators may tell you, the ideal combination of style, practicality, and comfort is rare. Making sacrifices to one or the other is inevitable. And using natural materials will not exempt you from compromise. However, choosing a natural material over a synthetic one may help you avoid the worst excesses of fashion and is likely to afford a more long-lasting tactile and visual pleasure in your interior.

FLOORING

The floor of a room has a profound effect, not only on its appearance but equally on its character and atmosphere. Natural materials are unbeatable for floors, which probably get more wear than any other

Today's living room is more like a Medieval hall than a Victorian drawing room or parlor; communal, informal, re-established as the space where family and friends gather to socialize and relax. As a room with many functions, private and public, its furnishings and finishes must bridge some awkward gaps—cozy enough to curl up alone with a book, hard-wearing enough to accommodate guests; offering a retreat from the world beyond the front door, and yet extending a welcome to chosen outsiders.

OPPOSITE PAGE: In this Hollywood house, living and dining areas are divided by a fireplace set into a slab of brickwork. Built in the 1940s and restored fifty years later by architect Stephen Slan, the furnishings encompass half a century of modernism, including a rare Edward Fields rug that marks out an area of warmth and intimacy on the concrete floor.
ABOVE: Living and dining areas merge in a London apartment designed by Brian Johnson, where a rug laid over limestone softens a seating area around a wood-burning stove.

THIS PAGE: A view from the living room of this light, bright house in Belgium by Paul ibens and Claire Bataille goes through to the television room. A wide strip of polished mussel limestone, flowing through the hall and up the stairs, separates the expanse of bleached teak floorboards. The adjustable antique work table, with its carved wooden screws, holds a still-life of slate-gray pots.

ABOVE AND LEFT: The living room of the same house uses a sophisticated combination of dove-gray and cream linen upholstery. The wicker basket of logs and the chunky stool by Christian Liaigre, complete with natural splits along the grain, add a dash of rustic innocence for a look that is as relaxed as it is elegant. White cotton slip-covers (left) are as fresh and pretty as a daisy chain.

surface in the house, because they tend to improve with age rather than deteriorate. Stone rubs into faint undulations; wood is worn smooth; even threadbare matting has a certain rustic appeal.

One of the reasons the floor has such a powerful influence over the feel of a room is the way it acts as a soundboard; battered by foot fall, scraped by furniture, reflecting and vibrating with ambient noise. A sprung wooden floor has a faint ring under the heel—bare wooden stairs are particularly resonant. Stone floors have a duller, more muted note. Matting absorbs sound, especially when padded by thick underlay, and deep wool carpet is quietest of all. Depending on its position in the house, the living room may be an area that is retreated to—as in most older houses,

LEFT: A concrete staircase by Bowles and Linares is elevated from the grimly industrial to urban elegance with the addition of a gracefully etiolated stair rail and banister.

BELOW LEFT: Balanced on the edge of a concrete hearth, a concrete bowl holds a trio of rubbed pebbles—further proof that concrete can compete with stone when it comes to looks and texture.

RIGHT AND OPPOSITE PAGE: If "texture is the new color," as interior designer Kelly Hoppen has opined, then this London living room (right) is a positive rainbow. An aluminum-framed sofa (near right) with thickly padded honey-brown felt upholstery holds pillows covered in a stretchy netting that looks like linen yarn, but is in fact bands of elastic, all designed by Bowles and Linares. A wicker screen and radiator (opposite) combine to form a room divider.

where it is separated from other rooms by a hall—or an area that is constantly crisscrossed to get to other rooms, a layout increasingly common in contemporary houses and loft-style apartments with open-plan arrangements.

The living room as retreat is well served by wall-to-wall carpet or, more fashionably, by matting. The most suitable mattings for living rooms are tough, hard-wearing coir and sea-grass. They can be laid wall to wall like carpet or as mats bound at the edges. The fibers of sea-grass are smooth and pleasant underfoot—although perhaps a little too knobbly for babies' knees—and are water- and stain-resistant. Their fresh smell, reminiscent of new hay, is an added bonus.

Leather floor tiles are an alternative that falls somewhere between hard and soft flooring—extremely expensive but undeniably luxurious, and exuding that inimitable scent of comfort and quality. Modern tanning and finishing techniques mean that leather floor tiles are surprisingly tough and resilient so, unlike childrens' shoes, will age beautifully, gradually acquiring that "antiqued" look that is so often badly faked on contemporary leather furniture.

THIS PAGE AND OPPOSITE:
Creamy colors predominate in Bernie de Le Cuona's living room and kitchen, where the textures of natural materials take center stage. Even the coal, glinting in its rough-hewn wooden box (right) has a tactile, natural beauty. Sofas are covered in heavy linen, and the pillow covers are also linen, dotted with leather buttons. The old stone fireplace is an almost perfect match with the newly laid flagstones. Between the sofas is a low African bench carved from wenge wood (below right). Also African are the wooden candlesticks on the mantelpiece and the leather Zulu skirts on the wall. A detail of a "tussah" or wild silk throw (far right) shows the slubby yarn that characterizes the threads unwound from silkworm cocoons gathered by tribespeople in the Indian jungle, quite unlike the smooth threads harvested from cultivated silkworms.

Two living rooms, one in London by architect James Gorst, the other in the Idaho mountains by architect Mark Pynn, both featuring wooden furnishings, wooden floors, and leather upholstery, for looks that are equally masculine but as different in flavor as oysters and apple pie. The two distinct styles of stone fireplace set the tone—refined, classical marble, discreet and tailored, for the London apartment, while in Idaho the room is dominated by a huge, rugged chimneybreast constructed from local stone.

Stone and wood are the most durable of all natural floorings, as the gleaming boards and marble hallways of many an old house can testify. Old wooden floors vary hugely in quality, from the cheap pine boards of attic bedrooms to the rich inlay of fine parquet. Even the most forlorn old floorboards can be coaxed back from decrepitude by sanding, filling, staining, and sealing, and the reward will be a floor that is original and unique. For an old house that has lost its wooden floors to blockboard, reclaimed wooden floorboards can restore character and a sense of history.

Once almost exclusively allied with the recreation of "period" interiors, wooden flooring is now just as popular in chic contemporary interiors; indeed an array of lookalikes, including laminates, veneers, and multilayer floorings have been developed as less expensive substitutes. You can even buy vinyl flooring that looks as though it has been freshly sawn. However, none of these alternatives are as hard-wearing as solid wood, and the laminates and vinyls miss out completely on the variety of color, shading, knots, and graining that make real wood so interesting to the eye.

Modern solid wood floors are usually factory-sealed or oiled so that no after-treatment is needed. Gaps and shrinkage are minimized, and there is a huge choice of types of wood, from the rosy tones and definite graining, of wide oak boards to the more uniform honey of beech. Wide boards, strong graining and dark knots create a more rustic look, while pale, faintly grained woods tend to look sleek and modern.

THIS PAGE AND OPPOSITE: For at least two centuries, the Indonesian rainforests have been plundered to feed a world hungry for the rich colors and grain of precious hardwoods. Recent concern over global deforestation has led to legislation to try to curb wholesale logging and encourage sustainable growth so that architects can again use hardwoods without harming fragile ecologies. The lavish use of hardwoods in these houses in Singapore contributes greatly to their sense of harmony with the nature beyond their windows. This seating area (opposite) is separated from the main entrance by a framework of wooden posts, centered on a panel of traditional fretwork. The house on the right has a living room with glass walls separated by sturdy wooden pillars that support a beamed roof. The result is a room that is fully engaged with its surrounding landscape.

Grandest of all is stone flooring, with its echoes of cathedrals, castles, and stately homes. As with wood, the aesthetic variations are myriad. Small, rounded tiles of tumbled marble look venerable, even ancient, while pale limestone is cool and contemporary. Riven slate, with its rippled texture, has a gentle, earthy look, while shiny granite can sparkle like a gemstone.

Few types of flooring are so versatile that they are equally suitable for every room in the house. However, allowing the same flooring to flow between rooms will make any space seem bigger

ABOVE AND RIGHT: Natural need not be neutral. Mary Shaw's Paris apartment is rich with color, its wooden paneling painted in shades from lavender to mustard, against which fabrics—woven wool and herringbone tweed—in dozens of colors are mixed and matched with abandon. Uniting them—aside from a discerning eye—is texture.

ABOVE: Clashing color in a cozy corner of the kitchen, where a sofa is draped with a tweed blanket and piled high with pillows and a soft braid-trimmed mohair blanket. The antlers are wittily echoed in the border below.

and more integrated. Instead of altering flooring between rooms, particular areas can be marked out for different uses or gradations of intimacy. In a living room that is also used as a passage to other rooms, a combination of hard and soft flooring is the most practical and appealing option. Hard flooring such as wood or stone serves best for thoroughfares, while matting, carpets, and rugs work well close to fireplaces and seating, where they create a sense of warmth and coziness, an intimate inner sanctum for kicking off shoes and lounging.

THIS PAGE AND OPPOSITE: Mary Shaw, the Irish owner of this grand Paris apartment, has achieved an amusing visual *rapprochement* between the two nationalities by furnishing its very French paneled and parqueted rooms with her own design tweeds of all descriptions. Plump Victorian armchairs are given a strangely modern twist when they are dressed in tight-fitting wool that would look just as much at home on a Scottish moor (left). Grounding the mix of colors, which range from burnt to bright orange, moss to lime green, is a golden patchwork of parquet that stretches throughout the apartment.

WALLS AND CEILINGS

Walls and ceilings make up the backdrop for an interior. Most modern homes use plaster and paint as a foil for paintings, mirrors, and furniture, but strikingly varied effects result when different materials are used.

Wooden paneling has a long history and was originally used as much for its practical insulating properties as for its decorative potential. At the height of its popularity, during the seventeenth and early eighteenth centuries, it was invariably painted, being constructed of inexpensive softwoods such as pine. Sometimes pine paneling was grained to resemble the hardwoods used for paneling in the most expensive interiors, but more often it was painted a flat color. Oddly, even the

THIS PAGE AND OPPOSITE: A layering of natural materials, a mix of simple modern pieces with plain antique ones, and a bold use of color characterize Roger Oates' and Fay Morgan's living room. Panels of rich red paint are picked up in the red wool upholstery and pillows. Linen drapes (right) hang in light layers of sheer and translucent color. The original pine floorboards, stained dark brown, are centered by a chunky woven abaca rug (above) with woven and felted wool matting overlaid for an even softer feel.

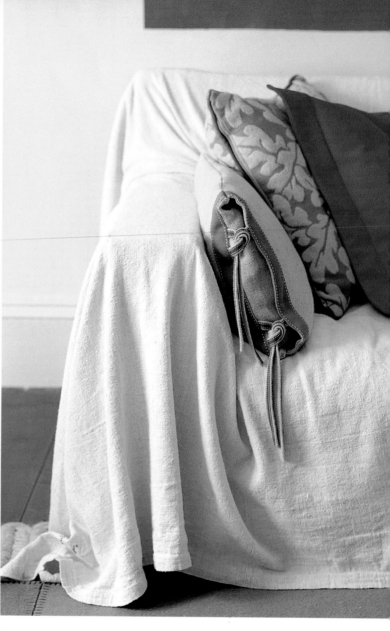

plainest painted wooden paneling—not so different, visually, from painted plaster—has a dramatic effect on the feel of a room, damping down the acoustics and bestowing an instant homeliness and sense of enclosure. However, modern wooden paneling is more likely to celebrate the warm colors and flowing grain of wood in its natural state. While wooden walls evoke cozy cabins, bare brick, or stone has a more raw feel, the bones of a building laid bare. Like unpainted wood, these are surfaces that need no additional decoration, providing enough visual interest in their unadorned state.

FABRICS

Fabrics provide welcome softness in any room and are particularly important in a living room, where we come to relax. Draperies are likely to be the biggest expanse of fabric in a room, and while the chintzy extravagances of the 1980s have been superseded by a taste for plainer fabrics, texture has now come into its own. Cotton, linen, wool, and silk have a distinct feel and drape, which can all

THIS PAGE AND OPPOSITE: The relaxed elegance of Roger Oates' and Fay Morgan's living room is partly due to the strict discipline of its palette, which is almost exclusively confined to the natural shades of natural materials—wood, wicker, marble, and unbleached linen—with the sole exception of bright, bold red, which partially covers the walls and appears in bright splashes as throw pillows. The sofa is dressed for summer (above), draped in a pair of antique French linen sheets. Before the mid-nineteenth century, when cotton began to take over, bedlinen, true to its name, was always made from linen yarn for rich and poor alike. However, the quality of the linen varied enormously—only the wealthy could afford the fine, smooth fabric that we associate with linen sheets and pillowcases today. Everyone else had to make do with a far rougher and coarser, even itchy, material which, although it makes an attractive and hard-wearing throw for a sofa, would be much less comfortable to sleep on.

be endlessly manipulated by ply and weave. Silk may be gossamer-fine and smooth as glass, or thick and knobbly as porridge; linen can be battered to the gloss of damask or loosely woven to make fibrous, translucent scrim; wool can be light as a feather or thick and weighty. Any weight of fabric can be suitable for curtaining, from gauze to tweed, depending on whether you want your curtains to filter sunlight and waft in the breeze or to provide effective draft exclusion and privacy.

Upholstery is a different matter, and requires a particularly strong fabric if it is fitted as opposed to a slipcover. However, pillows can be more delicate, and you can enjoy playing with contrasts of texture—velvet pillows on a leather chair, suede ones on a raw silk sofa. And, unlike clothes, which need washing and ironing with boring regularity, curtains, pillows, and sofa covers—barring nasty accidents—don't need to be thrown in the washing machine, so you can afford to ignore the temptations of easy-care synthetics and indulge in the undeniably superior sensual pleasures of entirely natural fibers.

"Natural fabrics provide welcome softness in a living room, where we come to relax."

OPPOSITE PAGE: Visual and tactile pleasures are provided simply and effectively. Cool cream cotton draped with a fine wool blanket for the sofa and a flat-weave rug over wooden boards mark this as an area of intimacy and comfort.
FAR LEFT: With its mix of elegantly simple wooden furniture and a restrained palette of neutrals spiced with strawberry, this is rustic style at its most sophisticated. Wall-to-wall coir matting is softened by the added layer of a chunky textured linen rug. Red "doeskin" wool covers the Knole sofa, which in summer is draped with an antique linen sheet.
LEFT: A feather pillow covered in an old linen grain sack makes a comfortable nest for Inca, the family dog.

THIS PAGE AND OPPOSITE: The bar, or half wall, loosely separating the kitchen from dining and living areas, is a modern must, as inevitable and desirable as a connecting bathroom. As a result, kitchen design has been encouraged to rise to the occasion—no longer hidden away in its own discreet space but on show. Wood, in this case oak, makes the link between the space for cooking and the place for entertaining with ease and grace, as practical as it is good-looking.

kitchens and dining rooms

The demise of the dining room is almost complete. Without an army of servants slaving over a hot stove, the separation of cooking and eating is an inconvenience. Instead of being relegated to the basement or the farthest wing, the kitchen is the hub of the modern house. For the experience of being waited on, we can visit a restaurant; to save time, we can buy a ready-made meal. Serious cooking, meanwhile, is a hobby, a leisure activity, a pleasure to be shared with friends.

The changing role of the kitchen is probably one of the most radical turnarounds in domestic architecture of the last century. Even fifty years ago, the fixtures and fittings of a kitchen were a low priority in most people's decorating budget. Today, as any realtor will tell you, the kitchen is regarded as one of the most important rooms in a house—its size and the quality of its storage space and appliances being key factors in its desirability.

Nowadays, perhaps the most coveted kitchen is the one where there is also space to eat. Best of all is the kitchen that is adjacent to a larger living and dining area, with a bar or a counter where once there would have been a dividing wall. Such is the new status of the kitchen, we prefer it to be on show. Once a purely functional space, the domain of servants and unacceptable smells, the contemporary kitchen is the equivalent of the old-fashioned dining room sideboard loaded with family plate—a symbol of wealth and success.

Building a kitchen is expensive. Despite this expense, it is the room most frequently renovated by a new house owner. And, despite the need for practicality and the fact that all kitchens require very similar combinations of storage, stove, sink, and refrigerator, kitchen design is particularly vulnerable to swings of fashion. Less than a decade ago, dragged paintwork in pretty blues and yellows with china knobs and cutout trefoils was all the rage. Today, the well-dressed kitchen has sloughed off frills and fuss in favor of a rugged, almost industrial rigor, gleaming with stainless steel and giant appliances.

While an acreage of polished metal may make you feel like a professional chef, for a room that will be as much lived in as cooked in, the high-tech approach can be clinical in effect—more

operating room than the place for a relaxed dinner with friends or a laid-back family breakfast. Using natural materials—oiled wood and polished stone—can soften the feel of the most streamlined kitchen without compromising practicality. Using the best-quality materials will also help to guarantee that the design of a kitchen will not date too quickly.

Wood and stone have always been the materials of choice for floors and surfaces in the rooms where food was prepared. Flagstone floors could be swept and scrubbed clean, and were less of a fire risk than wooden boards. A pine table could be scoured and bleached and used as a surface for chopping and cutting without blunting sharp steel knives. Cool marble slabs made the perfect smooth surface for rolling out pastry, and pantries were lined with slate shelving. Wood and stone continue to be favored for kitchens for some of the same reasons, while modern silicone sealants for stone, and oils and varnishes for wood, mean that both materials are easier to maintain than ever before.

THIS PAGE AND OPPOSITE:
Bright white spaces for
eating are a far cry from
the traditional dining room.
Formal dining today tends
to be confined to special
occasions or to restaurants
where we can enjoy the
pleasures of being waited
upon without employing
an army of servants. Simple
and unpretentious, these
tables are a blank canvas
ready to be painted in with
dishes, flatware, and food.
A cast concrete bowl by
Bowles and Linares (left
and below) is a foil for the
shapes and colors of fruit.
Vibrant interior greenery
(right) surrounds a table,
giving a fresh, conservatory
feel to the dining area of
this converted banana
warehouse in Belgium.

OPPOSITE PAGE AND RIGHT:
The simple, even stark, geometry of the dining room in this Belgian house by Paul ibens and Claire Bataille is softened by the warm colors and feel of natural materials. Sliding cream cotton blinds screen a window onto the hall, one wall of which is glass and overlooks the garden. The floor is bleached teak. Ranged around the custom-made dining table of stained oak planks, the dining chairs (right) have wooden frames covered with woven cane, taken from an original design by Jean-Michel Frank.

ABOVE: Another dining room with a view, this time of a London roof terrace. The dining table is lower than usual to allow a more relaxed way of eating and lounging. The Wishbone chairs are a classic Hans Wegner design dating from the 1950s. The limestone floor tiles that run through the apartment are left bare around the table for ease of cleaning, helping to distinguish this space from the adjacent seating area with its wool rug.

FLOORING

The flooring in a kitchen and dining area needs to be stain- and water-resistant and easy to clean. Wood and stone are equally suitable as long as they have been treated with appropriate sealants to minimize porosity. Stone needs added protection in kitchens, where it is vulnerable to fat and oil stains. Sandstone, which has large grains and pores, is not recommended for kitchens even when sealed, because grease marks may be impossible to remove. Slate, on the other hand, is particularly suitable due to its low porosity and resistance to acid.

A common objection to stone is that it will feel cold underfoot. In fact, as anyone who has tried to walk barefoot on a summer pavement knows, stone retains and seems to magnifiy ambient temperature very effectively. This quality can be exploited by the use of underfloor heating, which spreads warmth throughout the slabs of a stone floor to make a giant and gentle radiator.

Wood is a bad conductor of heat, but it is a good insulator, and, although it will not heat up in the same way as stone, neither will it make you wince with cold. Wood is more forgiving than stone in other ways, too; a glass may roll if dropped on wood, while it will surely break on stone. But wood may splinter, while stone will rarely chip. These are all qualities that must be taken into consideration before a final choice is made.

ABOVE, RIGHT AND OPPOSITE: When architect Stephen Slan took on the restoration of this mid-twentieth-century house in the Hollywood Hills, he replaced the original vertical wooden paneling with broad, horizontal redwood planks that wrap the dining area in glowing color. The floor is polished concrete with a look and feel like stone, and is separated from the walls by an angled, inch-high steel channel that gives the illusion of a gap, as if the walls were floating. The furnishings are plywood and in period: vintage Charles Eames DCW chairs set around a custom-made dining table designed by William Alexander, their curves echoed in the abstract that leaps out from the end wall. Glass doors open onto the surrounding garden.
LEFT: Horizontal iroko wood planks wall the galley kitchen of a London apartment designed by Brian Johnson.

SURFACES

The surfaces on which we prepare and eat our food should be hard-wearing, hygienic, and pleasant to the touch. Wood and stone, again, are favorite materials for kitchen work surfaces and have yet to be bettered by synthetic substitutes. The perfect work surface must combine qualities and withstand batterings beyond the capabilities of almost any single material: it must be wipe-clean, heat-, and waterproof, stain-resistant, and scratch-proof. Many people opt for a combination of work surfaces—chopping and pastry boards, heatproof mats and trivets—to accommodate these different requirements.

Wood is often chosen for both its look and its feel—durable, yet gentle to the touch. Close-grained hardwoods tend to be the most practical, and many have particular attributes; maple scrubs clean and doesn't taint food; elm is so water-resistant it was once

THIS PAGE AND OPPOSITE:
This contemporary house by Mark Pynn in the Idaho mountains has been built in the 'lodge' style, a rustic vernacular that characterized the architect-designed houses of the Great Camps in the Adirondack Mountains built during the late 1880s as country retreats for wealthy families. The Arts and Crafts aesthetic, with its emphasis on the "honest" skills of carpentry, is continued into the interior of the house with detailing like the square checkerboard raised panels of the kitchen cabinets, repeated at the corners of each window frame and magnified in the grid of the multipane sash windows and the glazed doors of kitchen wall cabinets. Hanging metal lanterns, designed by the architect, have an appropriately period feel, as does the stained pine Mission-style dining table. The high-backed oak chairs are copies of originals by Gustav Stickley.

used to build water pipes; teak is exceptionally resistant to decay because of its high resin content; oak is particularly hard. However, wooden work surfaces must be protected from extremes of heat, and spillages must be wiped immediately, as even well-oiled wood will soak up moisture that is left to stand.

Stone is, needless to say, tougher than wood. Less porous types of stone such as limestone, slate, and granite make kitchen work surfaces that can survive all manner of ill-treatment. Toughest of all is polished granite, formed from magma cooling slowly far below the earth's crust. While pale granites—white, gray, and yellow varieties—may mark, darker stones are almost stainproof. Unlike other kinds of stone, granite needs no sealant, as it polishes to a mirrorlike sheen, a process that transforms its matte, granular surface into a micromosaic of shiny crystals.

The other most important surface in a kitchen and dining room is that from which we eat. The softness and warmth of wood make it the ideal material for a dining table—a fact that seems so obvious, thanks to generations of usage, that we scarcely think about it until we try out an alternative.

THIS PAGE AND OPPOSITE:
The sleek kitchen of this
London apartment by
architect James Gorst was
built in a space formerly
occupied by a corridor,
necessitating a separate
dining room (above and
left). Linking them is the
reclaimed parquet floor.
The circular "Gouvernail"
mahogany dining table
and its matching chairs,
upholstered in glossy red
or mustard leather, are by
Philippe Hurel, and stand
on a thick wool rug. The
slate sculpture in the
corner is by Charlie Hull.
Although small, the
kitchen (right) exudes a
luxury that owes little to
modern gadgetry and
everything to its lavish use
of exotic natural materials:
black Turkish marble,
polished smooth for work
surfaces and walls, and
burl oak veneer for
cabinets. The effect is of
restrained exravagance,
like the interior of a grand
Art Deco ocean liner.

THIS PAGE AND OPPOSITE: The architect of these two houses in Idaho has almost exclusively used natural materials, giving the buildings an organic quality and making them seem at one with their landscape—"of a hill" as opposed to "on a hill," as Frank Lloyd Wright put it. The dry stone walling confers a monumental solidity on the interiors. Complementing the rugged feel of the stonework, natural wood, smooth and mellow, covers roofs and floors and serves as shelving. The kitchen and dining areas are linked by the common thread of these materials—granite for work surfaces; birch and natural-grain fir for cabinet doors in the kitchen, which flow into the stone walls and wooden beams that form a backdrop for dining.

Glass or metal, for example, may have much visual appeal, but the clatter of dishes and flatware on these cold, resonant planes can jangle the nerves in a way that is hardly conducive to digestion. Place-mats of some more yielding material can help to soften the effect, but the chilly edge of a slab of glass or steel is not the most welcoming place to rest a wrist or elbow.

FURNISHINGS
Wood and stone go together like sky and sea: whatever their respective colors or graining, they never clash, but instead seem to complement one another, the qualities of each enhanced by

> **Wood and stone have ancient links with the rituals of cooking.**

THIS PAGE AND OPPOSITE: There is an indefinable, universal pleasure in eating outdoors, be it a simple picnic on a rug, or dinner al fresco with candles and napkins. These dining areas in Singapore houses maximize the blurring of boundaries between indoors and outdoors, affording shade and protection from the sun while minimizing the sense of separation from nature. The more formal dining room (right) has floor-to-ceiling windows and French doors that open one whole wall of the room to the surrounding patio, with its geometry of dry stone walling (above) softened by the leaves of giant ferns and palms. The dining area opposite enjoys a position in that perfect space between interior and exterior, the veranda, shaded from the glare of the sun by fine cane blinds. The tables and chairs are antique Chinese.

contrast and comparison. Like all natural materials, they carry their own associations—wood and stone in particular have ancient links with the rituals of cooking and eating: stone for hearths and fireplaces, wood for vessels and platters. Quite aside from their practical advantages, these associations make wood and stone particularly appealing materials for rooms where we cook and eat.

The current trend in kitchen design is for a pared-down look with minimal detail. Aside from being fashionable, this is also entirely practical for a room where crumbs proliferate and damp dust sticks: the fewer nooks, crannies, and moldings in a kitchen, the easier it is to keep clean. Totally unadorned planes of glossy metal or laminate have their own ascetic appeal, but for a warmer, more homey look, natural wood adds color and subtle patterning to the plainest of designs. Cabinet doors sawn from burl oak achieve a refined, decorative richness due to the swirl and shading of the intricate grain.

The successful visual integration of kitchen and dining areas often relies on the use of related materials. As discussed in the previous chapter, allowing the same flooring to flow, in this instance between cooking and eating areas, makes an important link between these distinct spaces. In the same way, a wooden dining table and chairs will complement each other and seem part of a kitchen that is primarily constructed from wood. Other natural materials, such as leather or cane for seating, and linen or cotton for napkins and tablecloths, will blend equally well.

The modern kitchen is full of machinery—microwaves, dishwashers, toasters, and blenders. Very high-tech kitchens tend to emphasize this gadgetry and seem antithetical to the mess of mixing and rolling and tasting and stirring that is the real pleasure of cooking. With their pristine glint of the laboratory, these temples of hygiene are even more inimical to the joys of eating. Traditional wood and stone need not look old-fashioned, despite their venerable history, and continue to provide a background against which the rituals of preparing, serving, and eating a meal can be fully enjoyed.

THIS PAGE AND OPPOSITE: The lower ground floor of Bernie de Le Cuona's townhouse is a single large room complete with sofas, open fire, and dining table. Bernie de Le Cuona hand-selected the stub oak from which the kitchen cabinets were cut, choosing to leave the intricate grain that marbles the wall cabinets undisturbed by paneling, moldings, or even handles. The work surface is hard-wearing, water-resistant teak, and the huge central butcher's block is traditional end-grain maple—resilient enough to withstand a lifetime of chopping and cutting. The metal and wood dining chairs were designed for use with Singer sewing machines.

Notions of nocturnal privacy are relatively new. Until the seventeenth century, even the wealthy often shared their bedrooms and even beds with servants and children. A measure of seclusion might be obtained by pulling closed the curtains of a four-poster, but these were primarily for excluding drafts, not other people. Throughout the eighteenth century, the custom in polite society was to use the principal bedroom as the venue for suppers, card parties, and informal receptions. Only in the nineteenth century did the bedroom emerge as a more secluded space, although the steady stream of servants creeping in and out to attend fires, empty basins and chamber pots, and fill bathtubs hardly accords with contemporary ideas of privacy.

The modern bedroom may double as a place to sit and read or watch television or eat breakfast as well as a place to sleep, but only for the family. Allowing a friend or acquaintance into your bedroom is a gesture of trust and intimacy. Barging into someone else's bedroom without invitation is likely to be regarded a violation of territory.

The status of the bedroom as a retreat, an inner cocoon where you can allow all social defenses to drop, means that its decoration can be highly personal. Unlike the living room, hall, or kitchen, the public parts of a house, the bedroom is not a room for display. It won't be seen by most visitors, so you can be as eccentric as you like when it comes to decorating it. This might mean painting gold stars on the ceiling or draping a four-poster with a cloud of fairytale voile. Or perhaps your dream bedroom is more like Heidi's hayloft—an attic eyrie with a breathtaking view.

Whatever your idea of the perfect place to sleep, it is certain to feature elements that you find particularly soothing and comforting—colors that are gentle and warm, textures and surfaces that are smooth and soft. All the bedrooms on the following

bedrooms

LEFT AND BELOW: Soft folds of fabric line the walls of this bedroom like linenfold paneling, heightening the sense that this is an inner sanctum. A dressing room of closet doors faced with exotic sapele wood veneer serves as an antechamber and leads into a bathroom.

If the house is a child's first universe, then his bedroom is a personal planet. Of all the rooms in the house, the bedroom is the most private and intimate. Children fortunate enough to have one of their own will invariably adorn its door with notices warning others to "keep out." As adults we may choose to share this exclusive domain with a partner, but it remains an area of the house reserved for a limited inner circle.

ABOVE: Built by architect Mark Pynn in the American "lodge" style, the bedrooms of this house in the Idaho mountains enjoy spectacular views that are unencumbered by curtains. The beams use traditional and contemporary wood-work techniques to create a roof strong and steep enough to endure heavy snowfall. The architectural emphasis on craftsmanship is reflected in the sturdy Mission-style furniture.

LEFT: Built in the late 1940s by modernist architect Carl Maston, this house in the Hollywood Hills has been newly paneled by architect Stephen Slan in sweet-smelling, richly colored redwood. Cork tiles are warm underfoot in the master bedroom and continue the theme of natural materials in natural colors, as do the period furnishings—a leather-upholstered chaise by Edward Wormley and an undulating screen by Charles Eames.
INSET FAR LEFT: Iroko wood paneling, also used in the bathroom, doubles as a sleek headboard for the main bedroom of an apartment in London by Brian Johnson.

pages rely on natural materials to provide these visual and tactile experiences: all share a color scheme that is calm—based around shades of white and shades of brown, injected with warmth by the rich neutrals of natural wood; and all use the feel and texture of natural materials to create rooms that seem to offer pleasures for the skin as well as the eye.

The kind touch of wood, polished smooth, makes it an appealing choice for a bedroom floor—a temperate surface for padding around in bare feet. A mat or rug around the bed may add to the sense of coziness, but wood is never freezing cold. Some of the bedrooms featured here also have wooden ceilings, one has walls paneled in wood, another has floor-to-ceiling closets with unpainted wooden doors.

ABOVE: In a house by architectural duo Paul ibens and Claire Bataille, the light, bright master bedroom is a paean to the beauty of wood—its floor an acreage of pale, untreated teak. An expanse of white wall frames an artwork devoted to this same material, its golden grain pockmarked by a random spattering of holes that look like the work of giant woodworm.

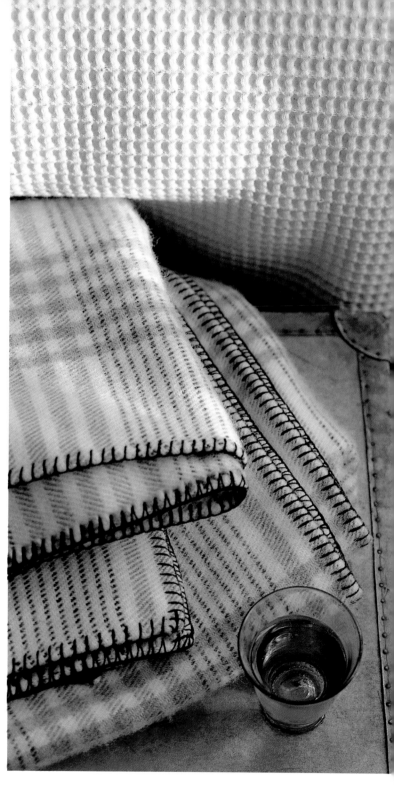

> *"Wood is the perfect material for a bedroom, where we need to feel warm and secure."*

In each case, the use of wood creates its own special atmosphere—a sense of being safely enclosed and protected. This is partly due to the evocative nature of this material, which has been friend to man for so many centuries, and partly thanks to its practical, insulating properties. Both are qualities that make wood a particularly appropriate material for a room where we need to feel warm and secure.

Wood has always been used for bedroom storage, from the earliest chests in which clothes were stored laid between dried herbs, through variations on the chest-of-drawers, which only made its appearance in the seventeenth century, to the banks of closets, shelves, drawers, and shoeracks that are features of so many modern bedrooms. Cedar has long been particularly prized for lining furniture that is designed to store clothes, as its resinous scent, which we find so attractive, is a very effective insect repellent.

Wood has an equally ancient history as the material of choice for bedsteads. The ancient Egyptians were the first to stretch leather straps or rope across a wooden frame to support a mattress, a design of bed also adopted by the Greeks and Romans, and still common in some parts of the world. The bedtime endearment "sleep tight" refers to a time when tightening the ropes of a bed was a regular necessity.

In the early nineteenth century, the predominance of the wooden bedstead was challenged by the introduction of mass-produced and relatively inexpensive iron bedsteads. At the time these were believed more hygienic than wood, as they were non-absorbent and therefore would not harbor "noxious miasma"—foul air, which was greatly feared as the principal source of disease. However, even fears for health could not persuade everyone to give up the cozy enclosure of a wooden bed—

THIS PAGE AND OPPOSITE: Two houses in the Idaho mountains built by Mark Pynn show different approaches to the structural problems of building a roof to endure heavy snowfall and, in the case of the roof shown on the right, also withstand possible avalanches. The ceiling on the left features a lattice of beams that is as decorative as it is robust and, where the roof rises to its apex, gives the bedrooms an architectural grace reminiscent of a Medieval barn or church. The roof treatment on the right looks more contemporary. Here, the strength of the steeply pitched roof is expressed in the deep buttressing of the ceiling. These bedrooms beneath the eaves call for little else in the way of adornment, decoration, or color, dominated as they are by the color, grain, and sheltering strength of this natural material, which has provided a roof over our heads from the earliest times.

a pleasure rediscovered in the recent revival of the *lit bateau*, a type of bed whose name and appearance make explicit the metaphorical links between floating in sleep and on water.

Probably the most important elements of comfort in a bedroom are provided by textiles—whether curtains to filter bright sunlight or block it out completely, or bedding, the second skin we cuddle up in before slipping into unconsciousness.

While heavy, luxurious drapes may seem appropriate in a living room, bedrooms require a cleaner, lighter feel. This preference appears to date back to the late Victorian obsession with minimizing dust in the bedroom, where contaminated air might harm the sleeper. This was a genuine concern in homes where coal fires produced a daily layer of fine black soot and at a time when cleaning heavy draperies was a matter of plenty of elbow grease and a carpet beater. Although much less of a practical concern today, the associations have stuck, and we tend to choose obviously washable fabrics for bedrooms as opposed to rich velvets or heavy woolens. Cotton voile is pretty and airy. Linen of various weights may provide more in the way of draft- and light-proofing while sharing that same freshly laundered feel.

Some bedrooms dispense with curtains altogether, but this is usually a luxury reserved for a house set in splendid isolation. But no bedroom would be complete without its bedlinen, whether it is a

THIS PAGE AND OPPOSITE:
Shades of pale make up
the bedlinen on Bernie de
Le Cuona's sumptuously
layered bed—a visual and
tactile feast of natural
materials. Purest white
linen pillowcases and
sheets, freshly laundered
and ironed, provide the
foundation. On top lie a
cotton knitted bedspread
and a wool-and-cotton-mix
paisley throw, all by De Le
Cuona. The square pillows
in front of the bed pillows
are knitted cashmere.
Leaning against the head-
board, which is covered in
tussah silk, are two square
pillows with linen covers.
Stripped pine floorboards
and a wicker bedside
table complete the scene.

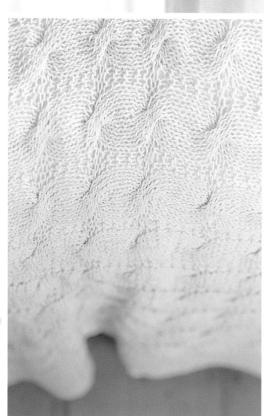

plumply padded comforter or the more traditional combination
of sheets and blankets. The weight, warmth, softness, and
cleanliness of bedclothes are all vital to the enjoyment of
bedtime and a good night's sleep.

As little as a hundred years ago, the luxury of clean, crisp
sheets could only be achieved as the result of a long and arduous
laundering process. If you were lucky, the filling of the copper
kettle, the plunging and swirling of the linen in boiling water,
the wringing-out, passing through a mangle,
hanging, and finally ironing, were undertaken by
your own servants. Otherwise, you could take
your dirty linen to the local washerwoman. The
alternative was to struggle with it yourself. The
washing machine has liberated us from this
backbreaking, scalding work only recently. It has
taken almost all the effort out of being clean and
doubtless made us less appreciative of the privilege
of fresh sheets. The ubiquitous cotton and polyester
blends that dominate modern bedlinen mean that
even the chore of ironing has been minimized.

However, while most of us today would balk
at an older generation's insistence on ironing
everything, including underwear, there is no doubt
that, in the case of bedlinen, pure cotton or, even
better, pure linen, scented sweetly from the wash
and ironed as smooth as marble is infinitely superior
to the touch than any of the easy-care options.
Sleeping on linen is a rare sensual pleasure, partly

INSET LEFT: Once reserved for sweaters and scarves, knitted
fabrics are now finding their way onto beds and sofas. As
cozy as the knitted crib blankets that some children turn into
comforters, the gentle swirls of this hand-knitted cable-stitch
bedspread make a rich textural pattern.

RIGHT: In this bedroom a sea-grass mat lies on top of a wool carpet, leaving a border of texture around the mattress. A piece of driftwood, a china cup, and a birchbark box make a tactile still life on the concrete hearth.

LEFT: Movable screens and white cotton curtains used as room dividers maximize the flexibility of the vast floor space in this converted warehouse. Futons with linen covers are laid on Japanese tatami mats on the sanded wooden floor.

due to the fact that its fibers are uniquely absorbent. Until the nineteenth century, when imported cotton became cheap and plentiful, linen was the only suitable material available for bedlinen and underwear, so rich and poor alike slept in linen sheets. However, only the rich could afford the type of fine, smooth linen we take for granted today, while everyone else had to make do with a much coarser, scratchier cloth.

By today's standards, linen is a particularly demanding fabric that creases and droops on contact, so a peaceful night's sleep can reduce sheets and pillowcases alike to a crumpled heap. To be experienced at its finest, linen must be fully laundered, lightly starched, and ironed every day. Unless you are fortunate enough to be able to pay for this service, the daily delight of fresh linen is simply impractical. Fortunately, crisp white cotton is a very close second to linen for an inviting bed and rather easier to iron, as well as being more crease-resistant.

Cotton and linen feel cool and downy against skin, but for warmth throughout a chilly night we need more insulation. The duvet, a Scandinavian invention that first began to oust sheets and blankets in other European countries and North America some thirty years ago, is becoming increasingly popular.

THIS PAGE: In this versatile interior, even paintings are propped (left) rather than hung, giving the sense that the furniture has no fixed abode. Wood dominates the decorative scheme, in shades that range from palest honey to chocolate brown.

THIS PAGE: An antique bed simply draped with inexpensive cotton voile transforms the top floor of Johanne Riss' converted warehouse in Belgium into a fairytale boudoir. The same gauzy voile drapes the windows, filtering and softening light, and affording privacy.

THIS PAGE: White, white, white—dazzling and delicate in a room that is both bedroom and living room. A mosquito net screens and encloses the bed, blurring its outlines. White cotton covers the sofas, white lace the pillows, and the wooden floor is bleached to the pallor of driftwood.

Filled with duck and goose down, the duvet combines lightness with a warmth that can only be equaled by piling on several wool blankets. However, the tactile contrasts between spongy wool and delicate cotton or linen and the heavier hug of a bed piled with blankets has its own appeal, a fact that is increasingly recognized by some of the world's finest hotels.

Even a duvet may merit the addition of a bedspread or throw, and here the opportunities for decorative effect and textural contrast are endless. Variations shown on these pages include a simple waffle-weave bedspread, a heavy cotton antique bedspread trimmed with lace, a simple folded blanket in fine orange wool, and, undoubtedly the most sensuous of all, a luxurious blanket of the palest, velvety suede.

A brown mussel limestone, mottled with fossil remains, creates a surprisingly warm feel in a sleek bathroom by Belgian architects Paul ibens and Claire Bataille. Where it has been used to surround the bathtub and line the walls, it is cut in vertical ribs, a detail echoed in the slats of the wooden Venetian blind. The same stone surrounds the twin sinks.

It is only necessary to live through a single morning without it to appreciate the marvel of hot and cold running water. One twist of the faucet and out it pours, clean, fresh, and clear, to fill the coffeemaker, boil the eggs, or wash the hands. Running a hot bath takes a matter of minutes. Flushing the toilet is a reflex action. In some parts of the world, however, water is still a precious, treasured commodity. The rest of us are very fortunate.

Bathrooms have become so important that we expect a new house with any more than two bedrooms to have more than one. And although, like bedrooms, bathrooms are private rooms, we lavish money on their fixtures, installing power showers, bidets, and double sinks and, where necessary, sacrificing bedrooms to give them the space we feel they deserve.

The current trend is for bathrooms that combine simplicity with the luxury and understated glamour of high-quality materials. Lining a bathroom with glossy, figured marble spiked with gold faucets may be an ostentation of the past, but the

Water has such a magnetic attraction it is easy to believe that we were once aquatic creatures. From stamping in puddles to shooting the rapids, we cannot resist playing with water—its sound, its power, its sparkle, and its feel on the skin. The bathroom is the room in which we indulge this age-old love affair.

best-dressed contemporary bathroom makes lavish use of stone to more subtle effect. Wood, once banished as a suspect for harboring germs, has made a comeback and is now being used for much more than just the toilet seat.

A large bathroom with windows and room enough for furniture other than the sort with faucets is a luxury, but even a small internal bathroom can be a sybaritic hideaway. Few physical experiences can compete for complete relaxation with

bathrooms

THIS PAGE AND OPPOSITE:
Despite appearances, the
only stone in this simple,
sensual bathroom is a
pumice stone. The large,
stone-colored tiles and
small mosaic tiles that line
the ample shower and
partially cover the walls
are actually porcelain. The
same tiles, with a matte
finish, are used on the floor.
And, while the sink looks
as though it sits in a slab
of subtly veined marble, its
surround is actually cast
from a secret recipe of
concrete, developed by
designers Sharon Bowles
and Edgar Linares. The
unusual light fixtures are
enameled metal.

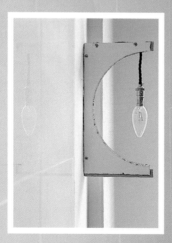

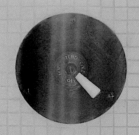

a long soak in steaming, scented water. Add music, candlelight, a good book, and a glass of champagne, and you have a recipe for guaranteed pleasure. Tottering, bleary-eyed into a big shower and pummeling your body awake with a torrent of warm water is a different kind of experience altogether, but a pleasure nonetheless.

Civilized life seems impossible without a bathroom, yet many of our grandmothers and grandfathers made do with a privy in the backyard and a tin bathtub in front of the fire. That familiar trio of bathtub, sink, and toilet, all conveniently plumbed in, with a room to themselves, was a rarity in Britain until the 1920s. Middle-class America was quicker off the mark, so that Edith Wharton could write of the "ordinary" bathroom in 1897 and how "the detached enamel or porcelain bathtub has in most cases replaced the built in metal tub." The British, however, led the race in toilet design, exporting their flushing inventions all over the world, including North America.

Before the democratization of piped water, bathrooms were either public, as in ancient Rome, or the privilege of great wealth. Contrary to their reputation—fueled by Queen Elizabeth I's famous claim that she had a bath once a year whether she needed it or not—Tudor royalty enjoyed the use of permanent, plumbed-in bathrooms at the palaces of Hampton Court and Whitehall. Throughout the eighteenth century, when France led the world in the field of interior design, all the grandest houses boasted their *appartements des bains*, often equipped with hidden tanks that could supply hot running water. Madame de

Pompadour had her bathroom lined with flocked wallpaper. Other designs of the period show elaborate draperies, curtains, and canopies, which gave these rooms more the look of grand living-rooms than the scene for ablutions.

By the 1890s, most city dwellers had a constant water supply with pressure that was adequate to reach rooms above the second-floor level. The modern bathroom was born, and for the first time, bathroom design and sanitary ware were big business. At first, bathtubs, sinks, and toilets were designed as if they were pieces of furniture, like washstands or commodes. Porcelain bathtubs and sinks were enclosed in carved and paneled mahogany, and toilets were similarly enclosed. The decoration of these new rooms was likewise very similar to that of other rooms.

As the links between dirt and disease became more widely understood, the emphasis on household hygiene grew. This new awareness of the dangerous potential of invisible germs encouraged the emergence of a more streamlined bathroom—pedestal toilets, sinks with iron fixtures, freestanding tubs that could be cleaned around and underneath—all in gleaming white porcelain or enamel—in a setting of waterproof walls and floors that could be wiped clean.

This is still the basic model for the modern bathroom and, while fashions in bathroom design have oscillated between cozy and colored, cool and clinical, some of the most important ingredients of the desirable bathroom have changed very little: as large a tub as practical, as efficient heating as possible, as high water pressure as feasible. And, despite having relaxed on the subject of germs, partly thanks to the battery of antibacterial cleaning agents now at our disposal,

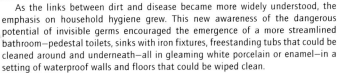

THIS PAGE AND OPPOSITE: Baby boulders of soap (opposite) in a bathroom that oozes luxury without breaking the bank. Designed by Bowles and Linares for a house in London using a neutral, natural palette, the room is a showcase for their creative brilliance with concrete. In the right hands, concrete can be a sophisticated substitute for stone, as this cast concrete sink surround (left) demonstrates. Also cast from concrete is the ribbed vase (above left). The faucets (above) have been patinated for a dark bronze finish.

THIS PAGE AND OPPOSITE: For a room where cleanliness is the object of the exercise, white, with all its associations of purity and hygiene, has a particular appeal. Like freshly fallen virgin snow, on which the lightest foot-print shows up as a mark, these are rooms designed to expose rather than accommodate dirt. Cotton towels provide softness in contrast with the flat, smooth surfaces of floors, cabinets and tiles. Fat, fluffy white towels, neatly stacked (left and bottom right) are the epitome of bathtime indulgence—spotlessly clean, promising a warm and absorbent hug for a wet body.

we continue to want to reflect the actual cleanliness of a bathroom in its design. As in the case of kitchens, a bathroom dominated by wipe-clean ceramics, metals, and glass can feel sterile, chilly, and inhuman. Natural materials such as water-resistant hardwoods and stone bring warmth and character to a room that can all too easily lack both.

Stone has an inbuilt aura of cleanliness—like mountains and waterfalls, it represents a type of natural purity. Unlike organic materials, stone does not decompose. Indeed, when appropriately sealed, stone is water-resistant, if not completely waterproof, and easy to clean. Water splashed on stone seems as natural as waves on a beach.

bathrooms 129

LEFT: Tucked in the corner of Bernie de Le Cuona's large bedroom, this is a connecting bathroom without the inconvenience of dividing walls. Bent copper pipes make a sculptural heated towel rod for a cotton terrycloth bath towel and woven linen hand towel.

"There are a few types of wood that are compatible with water."

Since man first learned to carve it, stone has been used to hold water, whether as rough-hewn troughs for animals to drink from or richly decorated vessels intended for religious ritual. Over the centuries, bathtubs, sinks, and toilet seats have all been carved from stone. Stone bathtubs were usually lined with linen cloths to take the chill off them and to soften their cool, slippery feel. Cutting-edge bathroom design has, in recent years, moved away from the built-in to favor free-standing tubs and sinks. This has led to a limited revival of stone sinks for home use. As expensive as they are beautiful, these bowls have an almost ceremonial presence, as long as you remember to hide the toothpaste.

Today in the bathroom, we are most likely to use stone for flooring, and for lining walls and showers. Limestone, granite, slate and marble are all suitable materials and, while pleasantly cool to the touch in hot weather, can be warmed through during winter months by underfloor heating. Stone can be equally effective for bathtub and basin surrounds and for bathroom shelving. When the same stone is used for floors and walls, the effect is seamless and integrated—minimalism without sensory deprivation.

Wood and water have a more adversarial and complicated relationship. All but the very densest and heaviest woods are buoyant in water, but almost all types of wood will rot and decay on prolonged contact with moisture unless they are adequately protected and cared for. While stone gently erodes, rubbed and polished over hundreds of years into smooth, round pebbles by the tireless attrition of the tide, wood may change character completely once sodden, swelling and disintegrating, losing its strength and beauty.

ABOVE AND OPPOSITE: In the same room, a raw silk throw covers the sofa. Linen curtains hang in two layers: one sheer, which can be pulled across for privacy, the other heavier, to screen the light. Hand-made soap, natural sponge, and brushes in wood and horn look almost good enough to eat (above).

OPPOSITE: Renovated by architect Stephen Slan, the bathroom of this Los Angeles house built in the late 1940s by Carl Maston retains a period feel, with its stylish and unusual mix of mosaic tiles, pale gray marble and dark wood drawer and cabinet fronts. The green of the tiles is echoed beyond the windows in the dappled colors of leaves and sunshine.
INSET LEFT: Ceramic tiles, wood, and marble, working in harmony.
INSET FAR LEFT: Teak, used here as a bathtub surround, is so water-resistant it can be used to make sinks and bathtubs.
THIS PAGE: In a London apartment designed by Brian Johnson, iroko wood paneling behind the bathtub creates a dark foil for a white tiled tub.

There are a few types of wood, however, which are compatible with water. Elm was used for water pipes until it was replaced by iron at the beginning of the nineteenth century. Oak, used for ships and barrels, retains it strength and structure when wet, although it will crack if it is allowed to dry out. Free-standing bathtubs were often made from wood, which is softer on the skin than the stone or metal alternatives. The Japanese, whose traditional bathing rituals are as strict on etiquette as their tea ceremonies, have always used cedar for bathtubs—after all, it is a wood that is waterproof enough for roof shingles, and releases its resinous aroma when it comes in contact with warm water.

Teak has a long maritime history and is often used for outdoor furniture, where its rich brown hue fades to a silvery gray. Even when its surface becomes slightly fissured and porous, due to long exposure to sunshine, the inner wood remains strong and impervious to water. Teak is so rich in natural oils that it can be used for sinks and bathtubs. Leakage will occur only if the wood shrinks to such an extent that the joints cease to be watertight. One way around this is to make the base of a tub or sink from laminated layers of wood that remain stable. A light surface oiling will bring out its rich grain, but otherwise teak is so strong that it can be cleaned as if it were ceramic.

THIS PAGE AND OPPOSITE: Early freestanding bathtubs of wood or stone, predating modern plumbing, were often lined with white linen cloths to make a gentler surface for the bather's skin. This contemporary version of an old idea in Roger Oates' and Fay Morgan's Georgian house converts an old-fashioned cast-iron rolltop tub into a shower, with cotton curtains hanging from wooden frames to form a canopy that also lines the tub. Wooden floorboards are covered with flat-weave rugs (opposite), and the capacious linen chest has wicker drawers (right) that complement the decorative wicker baskets. The effect is of timeless, almost monastic, simplicity.

Curtains can seem oddly inappropriate in a bathroom, even though this is the room above all others where we desire privacy and hate drafts. However spacious and well ventilated the space, some condensation is unavoidable in a bathroom, so heavy, thick drapes that may absorb moisture, and at worst harbor mold, are not practical. Frosted glass windows are perhaps the least fussy way to provide privacy. Venetian blinds are another effective and unfussy way to filter light and screen views, and are particularly attractive in wood.

This is not to say that fabrics have no role to play in a bathroom. On the contrary, a bathroom without towels is as cheerless and unwelcoming as a bed with a bare mattress. Like bedlinen, towels come into direct contact with our skin. But it isn't enough for a towel to be soft—silk velvet and duchess satin are as soft as fresh rose petals, but we wouldn't want our towels made from either of these fabrics. Towels must be soft, warm, and, above all, absorbent. This is why the very sight of fat, fluffy, cotton terrycloth is so appealing—it looks as though it will soak up a lot of water. Linen is even more absorbent than cotton—a quality that can be amplified by using a three-dimensional waffle weave—but linen towels are more an acquired taste, since they lack that fluffy plumpness that seems to promise warming and drying qualities combined. And why are towels so particularly appealing in white? It must be a resurgence of that paranoia about bathroom germs, for even the faintest smudge of dirt shouts its presence on a snowy towel.

THIS PAGE AND OPPOSITE:
Stone and water have an
affinity in nature that
translates well into a
domestic setting. Opulent
marble bathrooms of the
gold-faucet variety are
a decorating cliché, but
contemporary bathrooms
like these in houses in
Singapore make a more
subtle use of stone,
featuring pale limestones
and faintly veined marbles
for a look that is luxurious
rather than ostentatious.
In the bathroom shown
opposite, the gentle brown
of the stone that covers the
floor and walls is picked
up and intensified in the
warm toffee of wooden
drawers and cabinets.
A more radical use of stone
(below) for a sculptural
sink designed by architect
Chan Soo Khian.

WOOD

Barrows
The Window Shoppe
365 Boylston Street
Route 9
Newton
MA 02459
617-964-4580
www.barrows1.com

Gothic Cabinet Craft
27-50 First Street
Astoria
NY 11102
718-626-1480
877-4-GOTHIC (877-446-8442)
www.gothiccabinetcraft.com

Furniture Factory of Belleville
1000 Carlyle Avenue
Route 161
Belleville
IL 62221
618-277-9663

The Unfinished Wood Furniture Store
206 Taughannock Boulevard
Ithaca
NY 14850
607-273-4233
www.unfinishedfurnstores.com

Northwest Fine Woodworking
101 S. Jackson Street
Seattle
WA 98104
206-625-0542
www.nwfinewoodworking.com

Nude Furniture & Custom Made, Inc.
255 Jericho Turnpike
Mineola
NY 11501
516-294-0404
www.unfinishedfurnstores.com

Hansen's Furniture
411 Fraine Barracks Road
Bismarck
ND 58504
701-223-2565
888-221-2565
www.hansens-furniture.com

The Wood Works
305 East Walker
League City
TX 77573
281-332-2216
www.wood-works.com
Specialize in high-end custom furniture.

T & M Woodworking
PO Box 630
Jeffersonville
NY 12748
914-482-5511
888-539-6838
www.tmbedroomfurniture.com
This store specializes in solid oak bedroom furniture.

LEATHER

Hansen's Furniture
411 Fraine Barracks Road
Bismarck
ND 58504
701-223-2565
888-221-2565
www.hansens-furniture.com
They specialize in leather upholstery and solid wood furniture.

Spinneybeck
6000 North Bailey Avenue
Suite 1
Amherst
NY 14226
716-446-2380
800-482-7777
www.spinneybeck.com
This store specializes in high quality, full grain upholstery leather available in seven hundred colors.

Medallion Furniture
430 S. Main Street
High Point
NC 27260
336-889-3432
877-714-1539 www.medallion-furniture.com
This store carries an extensive selection of top quality home furnishings. They feature Italian leather by Nicoletti, German leather by W. Schillig, Canadian leather by Jaymar rattan furniture by Far East Rattan.

Brown's Leather Upholstery
3105 Sulphur Springs Road
Hickory
NC 28601
828-441-0664
877-336-5332
www.brownsleather.com
They specialize in leather furniture made with top grain leathers dyed all the way through the hide. They offer hundreds of colors and types of leather.

Leather Expressions
2217 Bristol Pike
Bensalem
PA 19020
215-638-3618
www.leatherexpressions.com
They specialize in leather home furnishings such as sofas, sectionals, chairs and recliners.

Blackstock Leather
13452 Kennedy Road
Stouffville
Ontario
Canada L4A 7X5
905-888-7070
800-663-6657
www.blackstockleather.com
This store specializes in leather upholstery and leather flooring.

Foremost Furniture
8 West 30th Street
New York
NY 10001
212-889-6347
www.foremostfurniture.com
They have a large selection of high quality traditional, contemporary and leather furniture. They also feature a professional design service at no cost to the customer.

Roden Leather Company
PO Box 555
Royal Oak
MI 48068
800-521-4833
www.rodenleather.com
They carry a wide variety of upholstery leather.

Leather Interiors
12605 E. Independence Blvd.
Matthews
NC 28105
704-841-0702
www.leatherinteriors.com
Specialize in leather furniture.

Signature Leather
712 Route 17 North
Paramus
NJ 07652
201-612-1001
or
127 West Kelly Street
Metuchen
NJ 08840
732-321-1100
www.signatureleather.com
Specialize in leather home furnishings such as sofas, sectionals, chairs and recliners.

STONE

Bedrosians
1235 South State College Boulevard
Annaheim
CA 92806
www.bedrosians.com
Specialize in first quality granites, marbles, limestone and slate.

Midwest Tile, Marble and Granite
200 West Industrial Lake Drive
Lincoln
NE 68528
402-476-2542
888-818-6864
www.midwesttile.com
Specialize in granite, marble, slate and limestone.

Short Hills Marble & Tile
658 Morris Turnpike
Short Hills
NJ 07078
973-379-4059
Specialize in high end antique stone. Also features Dolomya marble.

Prestige Bath & Tile
11 John Street
North Aurora
IL 60542
630-801-8600
www.annsacks.com

Stone Brokers of America
7790 N.W. 32nd Street
Miami
Florida 33122
305-593-8082
email: stonebrokr@aol.com
Specialize in fine natural stones.

Elon Tile & Marble
153 Main Street
Mr. Kisco
NY 10549
914-242-8434
email: elon@bestweb.net

Hastings
Tile & Il Bagno Collection
30 Commercial Street
Freeport
NY 11520
516-379-3500
800-351-0038
www.hastingstilebath.com

Ointon & Color Stone International
5475 Tulane Drive
Atlanta
GA 30336
4040-699-1937
www.colorstoneintl.com

Great Wall Granite & Natural Stones Corp.
239 Leslie, Suite C
St. Louis
MO 63021
636-256-9000
888-627-6888
email:greatwal@swbell.net

Galaxy Stone
122 Pittsburg Street
Dallas
TX 75207
214-741-6722
877-290-3924
www.stonesofindia.com

NATURAL FIBERS

Organic Cotton Alternatives
3120 Central Avenue SE
Albuquerque
NM 87106
505-232-9667
888-645-4452
www.organiccottonalts.com

**Soaring Heart Futon &
Natural Bed Company**
101 Nickerson Street
Seattle
WA 98109
206-282-1717
877-288-1717
www.soaringheart.com

Earthsake
2076 Chestnut Street
San Francisco
CA 94123
415-441-2896
www.bayarea.citysearch.com

Natural Spaces
6333 Macadam Avenue
Portland
OR 97201
877-877-4929
www.naturalspaces.com
*Specialize in natural fiber and
organic bed and table linens.*

La Musa
5345 Wisconsin Avenue NW
Washington DC 20015
202-537-5000
www.lamusa.com

Sisal Rugs Direct
PO Box 313
Excelsior
Minnesota 55331
888-613-1335
www.sisalrugs.com

**Cartozian Fine Carpets &
Rugs**
3320 South G Street
Tacoma
WA 98408
253-474-8433
800-499-9686
www.cartozian.com

Sibylla
31 Market Street
Saugerties
NY 12477
914-246-9710
888-742-9552
www.sibylla.com

**Pure Natural Fiber Clothing
& Goods**
At The Tannery Mill
50 Water Street
Newburyport
MA 01950
978-462-5999
www.puregoods.com

B & J Fabrics
263 W. 40th Street
New York
NY 10018
212-354-8150
*This store carries high-end
natural fabrics.*

Conrad Imports Inc.
San Francisco
CA 94123
415-626-3303
www.conradshades.com
*Available though designers
and architects.*

Environmental Home Center
4th Avenue S.
Seattle
WA 98134
www.enviresource.com

ARCHITECTS AND DESIGNERS
whose work is featured in
this book:

**Claire Bataille & Paul ibens
Design NV**
Architects
Vekestraat 13 Bus 14
2000 Antwerpen
Belgium
t. +32 3 231 3593
f. +32 3 213 8639
*20–21, 28–29, 37 b, 39, 53 r,
61 t, 68, 69 t, 86, 92, 93, 111*

Bowles & Linares
32 Hereford Road
London W2 5AJ
t. 020 7229 9886
*70–71, 88–90, 90–91, 118 tl &
r, 124–127*

Aude Cardinale
Designer
12 Avenue de Madrid
92000 Neuilly
France
*1, 8 r, 9, 13 r, 17, 19 tc, 36, 40,
42 tr, 46–47, 64–65*

**De Le Cuona Textile and
Home Collection**
Head Office:
9–10 Osborne Mews
Windsor SL4 3DE
email:bernie@softech.co.uk
www.delecuona.co.uk

Retail Outlet:
De Le Cuona
1st floor
The General Trading Company
Sloane Square
144 Sloane Street
London SW1X 9BL
*Endpapers, 6, 16 l, 25 tl,
48–51, 60 l & r, 72–73,
106–107, 116–117, 130–131*

James Gorst Architects
35 Lambs Conduit Street
London WC1N 3NG
t. 020 7831 8300
*8 l, 13 l, 14 tl & c, 22–23, 30
br, 42 l, 42–43, 43, 74, 75 tl &
bl, 98–99, 108, 133 inset l*

Johnson Naylor
13 Britton Street
London EC1M 5SX
t. 020 7490 8885
f. 020 7490 0038
*2–3, 18, 20 l, 44 l, 60–61,
92–93, 94 bl, 110 tl, 133 main*

Juan Peck Foon
Resources + Planning Design
Consultants
73 Cardiff Grove
Singapore 558939
t. +65 382 4518
f. +65 382 4865
*email:peckfoon@singnet.com.sg
14 b*

Roger Oates Design
The Long Barn
Eastnor
Ledbury
Herefordshire
HR8 1EL
t. 01531 631611
*7 tl & tr, 25 tr, 52, 53 l & c, 54,
55 tl, bl & br, 67, 82–85, 86–87,
87, 104–105, 112–113, 134–135*

**Mark Pynn A.I.A.
McMillen Pynn Architecture
L.L.P.**
P.O. Box 1068
Sun Valley, Idaho 83353
USA
t. +1 208 622 4656
f. +1 208 726 7108
email:mpynn@sunvalley.net
www.sunvalleyarchitect.com
*7 b, 14 tr, 15, 21 tl, 34, 35, 41
r, 75 r, 96–97, 100, 100–101,
101, 109 t, 114, 115*

Johanne Riss
Stylist, designer and fashion
designer
35 Place du Nouveau Marché
aux Graens
1000 Brussels
Belgium
t. +32 2 513 0900
f. +32 2 514 3284
*32–33, 56–59, 69 b, 91, 118
bl, 119–121, 128–129*

SCDA Architects
10 Teck Lim Road
Singapore 088386
t. +65 324 5458
f. +65 324 5450
email:scda@cyberway.com.sg
*10–11, 19 tr, 19 b, 27 tl & bl,
31 tr, 137 l & r*

Sequana
64 Avenue de la Motte
Picquet
75015 Paris
France
t. +33 1 45 66 58 40
f. +33 1 45 67 99 81
email:sequana@wanadoo.fr
25 br, 55 tr, 62–63, 78–81

**Stephen Slan, AIA.
Variations In Architecture Inc**
2156 Hollyridge Drive
Los Angeles
California 90068
t. +1 323 467 4455
f. +1 467 6655
*19tl, 37 t, 44–45, 45, 66,
66–67, 94–95, 95, 110–111,
132, 133 inset r*

source directory

KEY   t = top,   b = below,   l = left,   r = right,   c = center

Endpapers Bernie de Le Cuona's house in Windsor; **1** Aude Cardinale's house near Paris; **2-3** Roger and Suzy Black's apartment in London designed by Johnson Naylor; **6** Bernie de Le Cuona's house in Windsor; **7 tl & tr** Roger Oates and Fay Morgan's house in Eastnor; **7 b** Philip and Barbara Silver's house in Idaho designed by Mark Pynn A.I.A. of McMillen Pynn Architecture L.L.P.; **8 l** An apartment in London designed by James Gorst; **8 r & 9** Aude Cardinale's house near Paris; **10-11** A house at Jalan Berjaya, Singapore designed by Chan Soo Khian of SCDA Architects; **13 l** An apartment in London designed by James Gorst; **13 r** Aude Cardinale's house near Paris; **14 tl & c** An apartment in London designed by James Gorst; **14 bl** Namly Drive house in Singapore designed by Juan Peck Foon; **14 tr & 15** Philip and Barbara Silver's house in Idaho designed by Mark Pynn A.I.A. of McMillen Pynn Architecture L.L.P.; **16 l** Bernie de Le Cuona's house in Windsor; **17** Aude Cardinale's house near Paris; **18** Roger and Suzy Black's apartment in London designed by Johnson Naylor; **19 tl** Media executive's house house in Los Angeles, Architect: Stephen Slan, Builder: Ken Duran, Furnishings: Russell Simpson, Original Architect: Carl Maston c. 1945; **19 tc** Aude Cardinale's house near Paris; **19 tr** Isosceles Land Pte Ltd's house in Singapore designed by Chan Soo Khian of SCDA Architects; **19 b** A house at Jalan Berjaya, Singapore designed by Chan Soo Khian of SCDA

Architects; **20 l** Roger and Suzy Black's apartment in London designed by Johnson Naylor; **20-21** A house near Antwerp designed by Claire Bataille and Paul ibens; **21 tl** Philip and Barbara Silver's house in Idaho designed by Mark Pynn A.I.A. of McMillen Pynn Architecture L.L.P.; **22-23** An apartment in London designed by James Gorst; **24 & 25 tl** Bernie de Le Cuona's house in Windsor; **25 tr** Roger Oates and Fay Morgan's house in Eastnor; **25 br** Mary Shaw's Sequana apartment in Paris; **27 tl & bl** Isosceles Land Pte Ltd's house in Singapore designed by Chan Soo Khian of SCDA Architects; **28-29** A house near Antwerp designed by Claire Bataille and Paul ibens; **30 br** An apartment in London designed by James Gorst; **31 tr** Isosceles Land Pte Ltd's house in Singapore designed by Chan Soo Khian of SCDA Architects; **32-33** Johanne Riss' house in Brussels; **34** Phil and Gail Handy's house in Idaho designed by Mark Pynn A.I.A. of McMillen Pynn Architecture L.L.P.; **35** Richard and Sue Hare's house in Idaho designed by Mark Pynn A.I.A. of McMillen Pynn Architecture L.L.P.; **36** Aude Cardinale's house near Paris; **37 t** Media executive's house house in Los Angeles, Architect: Stephen Slan, Builder: Ken Duran, Furnishings: Russell Simpson, Original Architect: Carl Maston c.1945; **37 b** A house near Antwerp designed by Claire Bataille and Paul ibens; **39** A house near Antwerp designed by Claire Bataille and Paul ibens; **40** Aude Cardinale's house near Paris; **41 r** Philip and Barbara Silver's

house in Idaho designed by Mark Pynn A.I.A. of McMillen Pynn Architecture L.L.P.; **42 tr** Aude Cardinale's house near Paris; **42 l, 42-43 & 43** An apartment in London designed by James Gorst; **44 l** Roger and Suzy Black's apartment in London designed by Johnson Naylor; **44-45 & 45** Media executive's house house in Los Angeles, Architect: Stephen Slan, Builder: Ken Duran, Furnishings: Russell Simpson, Original Architect: Carl Maston c. 1945; **46-47** Aude Cardinale's house near Paris; **48-51** Bernie de Le Cuona's house in Windsor; **52 & 53 l & c** Roger Oates and Fay Morgan's house in Eastnor; **53 r** A house near Antwerp designed by Claire Bataille and Paul ibens; **54 & 55 tl, bl & br** Roger Oates and Fay Morgan's house in Eastnor; **55 tr** Mary Shaw's Sequana apartment in Paris; **56-59** Johanne Riss' house in Brussels; **60 l & r** Bernie de Le Cuona's house in Windsor; **60-61** Roger and Suzy Black's apartment in London designed by Johnson Naylor; **61 t** A house near Antwerp designed by Claire Bataille and Paul ibens; **62-63** Mary Shaw's Sequana apartment in Paris; **64-65** Aude Cardinale's house near Paris; **66 t & b & 66-67** Media executive's house house in Los Angeles, Architect: Stephen Slan, Builder: Ken Duran, Furnishings: Russell Simpson, Original Architect: Carl Maston c. 1945; **67** Roger and Suzy Black's apartment in London designed by Johnson Naylor; **68 & 69 t** A house near Antwerp designed

by Claire Bataille and Paul ibens;
69 b Johanne Riss' house in Brussels;
70–71 A house in London designed by Bowles and Linares; **72–73** Bernie de Le Cuona's house in Windsor;
74 & 75 tl & bl An apartment in London designed by James Gorst; **75 r** Philip and Barbara Silver's house in Idaho designed by Mark Pynn A.I.A. of McMillen Pynn Architecture L.L.P.; **78–81** Mary Shaw's Sequana apartment in Paris;
82–85 Roger Oates and Fay Morgan's house in Eastnor; **86** A house near Antwerp designed by Claire Bataille and Paul ibens;
86–87 & 87 Roger Oates and Fay Morgan's house in Eastnor; **88–90 & 90–91** A house in London designed by Bowles and Linares; **91** Johanne Riss' house in Brussels;
92 A house near Antwerp designed by Claire Bataille and Paul ibens; **92–93** Roger and Suzy Black's apartment in London designed by Johnson Naylor; **93** A house near Antwerp designed by Claire Bataille and Paul ibens;
94 bl Roger and Suzy Black's apartment in London designed by Johnson Naylor;
94 tl, 94–95 & 95 Media executive's house house in Los Angeles, Architect: Stephen Slan, Builder: Ken Duran, Furnishings: Russell Simpson, Original Architect: Carl Maston c. 1945; **96–97** Philip and Barbara Silver's house in Idaho designed by Mark Pynn A.I.A.

of McMillen Pynn Architecture L.L.P.;
98–99 An apartment in London designed by James Gorst; **100** Richard and Sue Hare's house in Idaho designed by Mark Pynn A.I.A. of McMillen Pynn Architecture L.L.P.;
100–101 & 101 t & b Phil and Gail Handy's house in Idaho designed by Mark Pynn A.I.A. of McMillen Pynn Architecture L.L.P.;
104–105 Roger Oates and Fay Morgan's house in Eastnor; **106–107** Bernie de Le Cuona's house in Windsor;
108 An apartment in London designed by James Gorst; **109 t** Philip and Barbara Silver's house in Idaho designed by Mark Pynn A.I.A. of McMillen Pynn Architecture L.L.P.; **110 tl** Roger and Suzy Black's apartment in London designed by Johnson Naylor; **110–111** Media executive's house house in Los Angeles, Architect: Stephen Slan, Builder: Ken Duran, Furnishings: Russell Simpson, Original Architect: Carl Maston c. 1945; **111** A house near Antwerp designed by Claire Bataille and Paul ibens;
112–113 & 113 Roger Oates and Fay Morgan's house in Eastnor; **114** Philip and Barbara Silver's house in Idaho designed by Mark Pynn A.I.A. of McMillen Pynn Architecture L.L.P.; **115** Richard and Sue Hare's house in Idaho designed by Mark Pynn A.I.A. of McMillen Pynn Architecture L.L.P.;
116–117 Bernie de Le Cuona's house in

Windsor; **118 bl** Johanne Riss' house in Brussels; **118 tl** A house in London designed by Bowles and Linares: Futon, The Futon Company/Mat, The Cane Store/Pillowcases and folded sheet, Muji/Suede throw, Alma Home; **118 r** A house in London designed by Bowles and Linares;
119–121 Johanne Riss' house in Brussels;
122–123 A house near Antwerp designed by Claire Bataille and Paul ibens;
124–127 A house in London designed by Bowles and Linares; **128–129** Johanne Riss' house in Brussels; **129 t** A house at Jalan Berjaya, Singapore designed by Chan Soo Khian of SCDA Architects;
130 l & 131 Bernie de Le Cuona's house in Windsor; **132 & 133 inset r** Media executive's house house in Los Angeles, Architect: Stephen Slan, Builder: Ken Duran, Furnishings: Russell Simpson, Original Architect: Carl Maston c. 1945; **133 main** Roger and Suzy Black's apartment in London designed by Johnson Naylor; **133 inset l** An apartment in London designed by James Gorst;
134–135 Roger Oates and Fay Morgan's house in Eastnor; **137 l** Isosceles Land Pte Ltd's house in Singapore designed by Chan Soo Khian of SCDA Architects;
137 r A house at Jalan Berjaya, Singapore designed by Chan Soo Khian of SCDA Architects

acknowledgments

The people without whose help and support I would not have written this book include my husband Richard, who proofread every word before everyone else; Dinah Hall, friend, colleague, and helpline; and Annabel Morgan, the book's editor, who has been a pleasure to work with. I would also like to thank the experts on wood, leather, stone, and natural fabrics who were so generous with their time and knowledge, in particular Fay Morgan of Roger Oates Design, Bernie de Le Cuona, Alastair Jessel from Stonell, Steve Maltby from Junckers, Charlton Clark from the Forestry Commission, Michael Whiteford from Bridge of Weir Leather, and William Garvey.